GREG & AMI

THE
AUTHORITY
OF
LOVE

All Scriptures in Preface are NASB. All Scriptures
in the rest of the book are NIV unless otherwise noted.

Disclaimer: All names in personal stories throughout
this book are changed for purpose of anonymity.

ISBNs
Print or paperback ISBN: 978-1-7362393-3-9
Kindle ISBN: 978-1-7362393-0-8
eBook ISBN: 978-1-7362393-1-5
Print or paperback ISBN, 2nd Edition: 978-1-7362393-5-3
Kindle, 2nd Edition: 978-1-7362393-4-6

Permission requests:
Contact Greg Williams at loveandlordship@gmail.com
or 859.229.6504.

Ordering information:
For bulk orders or quantity discounts, contact Greg
Williams at loveandlordship@gmail.com or 859.229.6504.
Includes any ministry or faith-based organization
that would like to partner with us to sell books
for 20% of net profits.

Printed in the United States of America.

Second Edition — August 2021

THE AUTHORITY OF LOVE

Greg Williams, Author
Ami Williams, Editor

This book and the Love & Lordship ministry are the result of years of teaching and mentoring men and couples in life and relationships. Our mission is to re-establish His Covenant Order through marriage and family and in all relationships. The vision is discipleship in loving relationships under the Lordship of Christ. We long to see these four tenets restored according to His Word, design and plan by the power of The Holy Spirit in Christ's Authority in His Church:

1. The Imago Dei (Image of God) with Christ as Lord in all things;

2. Agape (Godly, selfless, sacrificial, unconditional Love) Marriages, Families and Relationships;

3. Relational Servant-leadership and;

4. Generational Discipleship in our homes, the Church and world.

This is God's Covenant Design for peace in our life, marriage, family and Christ's Church to impact our chaotic culture and world for His Kingdom.

"

Just this week, week seven of the imposed coronavirus quarantine, I was asked by a fellow Christian leader, 'Other than the Bible, what book have you read during this extended period of isolation at home that has been most personally inspirational?'

My answer was, Love and Lordship's "The Authority of Love" by my friend, Greg Williams.

It is Biblical, clear, transparent and relevant:

- Books that are intended to be discipling tools, especially for men, must have the authority of God's Word laced into the text. Men will pay attention when God is allowed to speak. The exposition of scripture and the illustrations from scripture underpin the content of the book at every turn of a page.

- Greg is a linear thinker... like me! His book is logical. There is no way to get lost chasing 'rabbit trails' because there are none. He lays a foundation and then moves us step-by-step down a path of understanding the motives and methods for becoming a more devoted disciple of Jesus Christ.

- I am not sure I have ever read a book in which the author has been as open and honest as Greg. His humility in sharing his life journey is both endearing and engaging. Again and again he draws us into his story, a story with which the reader will easily identify.

- Greg is not an ivory-tower theologian. He is a down-to-earth practitioner of faithful Christian living. "The Authority of Love" is in touch with the real 'world, flesh and devil' and how each seeks to threaten and corrupt our daily walk with Christ.

[Don't start reading this book at 10:00 PM at night! You may find yourself groggy from lack of sleep the next day...]"

— Dr. Ken Idleman, Former President,
Ozark Christian College (1979 – 2006)
V.P. of Leadership Development for The Solomon Foundation

Greg's passion for the Lord, His Word and his own family
is the actual force behind this book. Like a vitamin supplement,
"The Authority of Love" is packed with Biblical truth and wisdom
that every family should have at its disposal. God's goal is healthy
families that thrive, not just in and for themselves, but for the
Lord and His purposes. Read the book, build these truths
into your own life and relationships and move forward
into the things that God created you to do."

— Kent Ostrander, Executive Director
The Family Foundation

I am delighted to recommend Greg Williams' latest book
"The Authority of Love." This book is grounded firmly in
Biblical principles for marriage, family and the Christian home.
These are timeless truths Greg has taught for many years.
He not only teaches but models them in his own life, marriage
and parenting. This book will be particularly helpful for
discipleship and small group studies. When I pastored a local
church Greg came and taught these principles. His lessons were
very well received and desperately needed in a day when
marriage, family and home are under attack."

— Wally Rendel, Senior Minister (Retired)
Jessamine Christian Church, Nicholasville, KY

I have gleaned from Greg's friendship for over a decade.
I love how he expounds the Scripture and weaves it tightly
into the principles of marriage. This book will not only encourage
your own marriage, but the small group study will give you the
tools to influence other men and women as well. Greg has done
a marvelous job of coupling his own experiences in marriage and
counseling with the Lordship of Christ in his own personal walk."

— Dr. Tim Turner, Director of Evangelism and Discipleship
WV Convention of Southern Baptist

FOREWORD

I've said many times that God knew what I needed in a husband way before I did. God knew I would need a strong man committed in the Lord to be my husband and the father of my children. Certainly, our marriage has not always been perfect but I know having Greg Williams as my husband was a part of His most perfect plan.

Every word in this book comes from a man whose heart truly beats for God. Greg not only loves His Word and seeks His will, he spends every day in conversation with Him. He constantly evaluates his thoughts and actions to make sure they glorify God and show love for others.

Since the day I met Greg over 30 years ago, he has had a passion for giving others the gift of Jesus' love and lordship in their lives. This book is a culmination of what truly gets Greg's heart racing: healthy men, healthy women, and healthy children in healthy relationships to the glory of God.

Our prayer has always been that God would work through us to share His message to reach others so they can experience the peace and freedom that can only come by seeking Jesus Christ as Savior and Lord.

— Ami Williams

CONTENTS

Section 4

Relationships: What We Were Created For

Section 5

Marriage: In God's Image

Section 6

Marriage, Family & Parenting God's Way

Section 7

The Home & Relational Servant-leadership in Christ's Family

Section 8

Wise as Serpents, Gentle as Doves

PREFACE

I've been asked hundreds of times over the past two decades, "Where are your books or DVDs?"

Well, here's the first, and maybe the last. I find it very interesting that the convergence of encouragement by several great friends, opportunity and timing, as well as years of preparation of my heart and mind come together at this time.

We find ourselves in the middle of the first global pandemic in a century as well as political and social upheaval in the USA like we've not seen in decades. In these trying times our faith is being tested. I believe God is calling Christ's Church to a spiritual awakening.

That awakening is not just to update church services, accommodating the culture, thinking we will reach more people. It is a call...

> For personal and collective confession and repentance of idolatry and compromise;

> For believers to absolutely make Christ Lord of every part of your life;

> For men to be Godly relational servant leaders, as husbands who love their marriage, spouse and family above their own success, glory and desires, just as Christ did for His Bride, The Church;

> For marriages to be a positive testimony to the Gospel of Christ so the world will see and know Him;

> To husbands and wives to submit to one another out of reverence for and submission to Christ as Lord;

> To disciple our children in our homes and, in all of the above, to build loving relationships that strengthen Christ's Church;

> To move beyond drawing people into a weekly one-hour service or a couple hours of weekly activity;

> To disciples to create loving relationships that hold each other accountable as we walk in His love and Lordship.

That call is the message of this book.

Without the Truth and grace in love of Jesus Christ, my Savior and Lord, this book would have been impossible and my life would be a mess. Thank You, Jesus, over and over again!

I must also thank my beautiful and wonderful wife, and editor, Ami. She is the light of my earthly life as we have walked this journey together in Christ. "An excellent wife, who can find? For her worth is far above jewels. The heart of her husband trusts in her, and he will have no lack of gain. She does him good and not evil all the days of her life." (Proverbs 31:10-12) You are such an amazing blessing to me and our precious children and all those who know you! Thanks, Babe. I'm truly a blessed man in every way!

Beyond that I couldn't have written this book without the blessing of my children. To our sons, Lansing and Harrison, I can't say it any better than this; "A wise son makes a father glad," (Proverbs 10:1) and my heart is very glad because of both of you.

To my precious princess, Haidyn, you have been the second most beautiful young lady I've ever seen. You are also brave and courageous, like your brothers, in standing up for what is right and I praise The Lord for your heart and courage. You are awesome! "Many daughters have done nobly, but you excel them all." (Proverbs 31:29)

All of you are incredible and I look forward to all that The Lord has in store for you. Ami and each of you have made it seem unbelievably easy and extremely rewarding to be a husband and father. Thank you so much!

I hope that you, the reader, will see that this ministry and message is a lifetime and a family in the making, and that it encourages and challenges you to surrender to the Lord and allow Him to do the same in your life, marriage and family for His Kingdom and Glory.

I must also acknowledge the following for their encouragement and feedback: My great friend, encourager and accountability partner, Greg Horn; My mentor and friend, Judge Tim Philpot; My friend and chief encourager in this book, Kent Laufenburger; My friend and mentor, Earl Ogata; My childhood friend (our dads sang in a Gospel quartet together for decades), Steve Kitts; My good friend and excellent reviewer, EG (you know who you are); and thanks to Jeff Hancock for his design work and to Jeff Rogers for his photography for the cover and our bio photo! I would be remiss if I did not also thank Kent Ostrander, Executive Director, The Family Foundation (KY) for his encouragement and for allowing Love & Lordship to be brought under their umbrella. Thanks so much to each of you for believing in The Lord's hand on me, and His work through me for His Glory.

I began writing just after celebrating the 60th anniversary of my parents, Elliott and Peggy Williams. Congratulations on a rare milestone that very few reach and an incredible testimony to God's faithful commitment in covenant love! I love you and thank you for your example to me and my family and so many others!

Far too often, nearly every man and couple that I counsel, mentor or speak with comes from a church background and has very little idea what Christ's Love and Lordship means according to His Word. They attend church and often are in a small group. Their children attend children's and youth ministry but their understanding of God's Word is lacking at best and usually nearly absent—and it is very evident in their marriage and family.

This is a wake-up call to the modern-day American church to place the priorities of discipleship in loving relationships—beginning with marriage and family in the home—above attendance, conversions, and success.

It cannot be just an occasional teaching on marriage as one man/one woman for life, but prioritizing it in everything that is done. It's teaching, building, and holding accountable young people and all people (those unmarried, married, and divorced) to the high standards of God's Word in relational and sexual purity and integrity. It is encouraging ALL to honor marriage (Hebrews 13:4) and to seek and extend the high calling of relational servant-leadership in Christ's Church to those who have lived accordingly (1 Timothy 3:4-5).

Love & Lordship, from which this book springs, is a ministry and message that calls those who claim Christ as Savior and Lord to model the image of God in these steps:

1) Christ as Lord in all things reflected in...

2) Loving Marriages/Families/Relationships that lead to...

3) Relational Servant-leadership in marriages and families that develops...

4) Generational Discipleship in personal life, family, the Church, and culture.

My prayer and desire is to lead people into a deeper relationship with Him, in their marriage and family and in all relationships, to strengthen His Church through His Love and Lordship!

Several authors are quoted in this book but none more than Oswald Chambers whom I have read every day for over 30 years. Other than God's Word, Chambers' influence has had the greatest impact on my spiritual life.

— Greg Williams

> *"Natural devotion may be all very well to attract us to Jesus, to make us feel His fascination, but it will never make us disciples. Natural devotion will always deny Jesus somewhere or other."*
>
> — Oswald Chambers, *My Utmost for His Highest*

INTRODUCTION

This is not politically correct, but I need to say it: if you're not serious about walking with Christ as your Lord and you as His disciple, building deep loving relationships in Him—especially marriage and family—this book may not be for you. I pray it is. If you are serious, read on! Also, it is deep and challenging! I recommend a chapter a day but that's your call.

"But make sure that in your hearts you honor (set apart) Christ as Lord. Always be ready to give an answer to anyone who asks you about the hope you have. Be ready to give the reason for it. But do it gently and with respect." (1 Peter 3:15 / NIRV) (parentheses added)

I grew up in a very church-going Christian family as an "all-American" kid. I got good grades, played the piano, sang in choir, played sports, and was sheltered from much of the world. My life consisted of church, family, school, farm and basketball—not necessarily in that order.

Ah, church! Well, that was just as much a success pursuit as anything else. In Sunday School class or Christian service camps we'd get a gold star for attendance, extra points for the number of Bible chapters read, and even more points for verses memorized. While I loved the little prizes we'd get and competitions we'd win, the best part was the recognition. Everyone "oohed and aahed" when I told how many chapters I read and how many verses I memorized. And with all those points my team could win! Awesome!

It all looked and sounded good, but it was rooted in my pride and flesh. Every win led to more prideful church service or volunteering in the community, which made the church—and me—look really good!

I spent much of college and a few years beyond thinking I knew more than God. I chose to do relationships and sexuality my own way and as long as I went to church with my girlfriend(s) and treated them nicely then surely God was OK with it. Partying was fine because everyone else was doing it. The enemy and world were all too willing to accommodate as I kept up the façade of the nice, all-American, Christian young man.

Whenever I stepped outside my own ever-expanding boundaries and felt a bit guilty I would simply show up at church, quote Scripture, have some spiritual conversations, worship, and enjoy a nice message— although occasionally the message would hit way too close to home. With my guilt assuaged I would walk a little straighter line for a while and eventually end up back in the same patterns and places. It was a cycle I could live with...for a while.

Along the way doors opened for several opportunities to pursue my dream of professional basketball—overseas and in the USA. Life was good and most anyone would have thought that I was a nice guy with a winsome attitude, athletic success, and a good heart!

God knew better.

He first got my attention at the Athletes in Action training camp in May 1987. Mike Sigfrids, Assistant Coach (and Discipler), explained on the first day of training camp that we were going to be playing world-class competition and pursuing our basketball careers on a four-month tour of what were then the Soviet Union and Yugoslavia but there was a greater purpose. He told us that we would be awakened 15 minutes early every morning and, although they could not and would not force us, they asked us to spend those 15 minutes reading The Bible, praying and meditating.

I fully agreed with Mike's comments about pursuing a basketball career; after all, I'd just returned from Ireland where I'd held basketball camps and toured with professional players with great success.

But God was up to something else. As I listened to Mike, The Lord spoke to me. He dropped these thoughts into my mind: "You think you're here to further your basketball career, but this is what you're really here for." I thought, "OK" and began to take to heart what Mike (and The Lord) said. I began that day in May 1987 to study God's Word daily, pray and apply that Word to my life. I have continued every single day for 34+ years in His Word, in prayer and time with Him.

I'd like to say the change was immediate but most of us know that The Lord usually works patiently through discipline over time...that's discipleship. He had my attention, but I was still playing the game of church while enjoying the fruits of sin, partying, imbibing, and indulging my fleshly desires.

God was faithful. He graciously and patiently broke me completely and captured my whole heart over the next 14-15 months.

Through a series of consequences brought on by my own actions, I found myself weeping on my bedroom floor in confession of my sins. As I wept I had a vision of a Roman soldier pounding nails into hands and feet on a wooden beam. As the camera in my mind panned out I saw Jesus' blood and tear-stained face and the Roman guard's face was mine. Hebrews 6:6 flooded into my mind!

Remember the "competition" of Bible reading, memorization, serving, etc.? While I did it for selfish, prideful reasons, God did not waste any of it! The verses, stories, and lessons came flooding back with new and renewed insight and power.

As I spent time in His Word and presence, He began to shift my thinking from professional basketball to pouring His love into young people, particularly boys and young men. Once again I heard God say to me, "I need someone to help raise up Godly men, marriages, and families because the enemy is wreaking havoc in these relationships and crippling My Church!"

So, right at the doorstep of realizing my dream of playing professional basketball, The Lord clearly guided me to help raise up Godly men, husbands and fathers—disciples of Christ.

I spent the next 14 years in teaching, coaching, and administration in public and private schools. I then shifted for eight years into directing a non-profit Sexual Risk Avoidance program and then transitioned into building the Kentucky Marriage Movement with The Family Foundation the last 10 years.

I had a mentor tell me that God has given me a story and by His grace I've won at marriage and family and that is why God has called me to speak to it. You will read stories and anecdotes throughout this book about our marriage and family as well as others that I've had the privilege to encourage, challenge and point to His Love and Lordship. Christ has saved us and given us His Holy Spirit so that we could be His witnesses to others (Acts 1:8).

This story was a pivotal moment where I died to myself for the sake of my wife, marriage, and family, ultimately to honor Christ. That is what each of us must do in discipleship and in our marriages and families. He must take priority and in order to do that, by His grace we must choose to decrease (John 3:30). That's how we become His witness...a testimony to His life in and through us!

During the early years of our marriage I was a high school athletic director and basketball coach. When I went to one school as a head coach, I inherited a team that was picked dead last and predicted to go 3-25 that first year. We won 12 games that first year and 16 the second, finishing third in our region. We were slated to be first in the region the next year with eight of our top nine players returning.

As we neared the end of that second season Ami found out she was pregnant with our third child, our precious Haidyn.

I knew that moving away from family and friends for this coaching job had been difficult for Ami as she was raising two toddler boys. They were very good but were "all boys." She had been a great support for me.

I approached her one weekend and asked what she thought we needed to do. We prayed and on Sunday evening she said she thought it would be best for us to move back where there was more family and friend support.

I went to my principal the next morning and resigned, knowing we had a potential regional, and possible state championship, contender. (That team lost by five points in the regional finals to the eventual state champions!)

Little did we know what God had in store. We moved back to Lexington and I took a substitute position that paid about half my previous salary with no benefits.

On October 1, Ami checked into the hospital with the largest major blood clot that two hematologists had ever seen. She was in the hospital for 23 days through two surgeries, the second being a C-section delivery of Haidyn on October 18, 1999.

There were seven specialists and seven nurses and assistants in the delivery room! Two healthcare executives that have gone through the Love & Lordship series said the bill would have been $500,000 - $1,000,000 but we never got a single bill.

A song by Avalon, "Can't Live a Day Without You," was #1 on the Contemporary Christian charts in October 1999 and I heard it several times a day. I wanted Ami to hear it as it had a double meaning for me: I couldn't live without Christ, but I also prayed and put it in His hands that I needed my wife and our two sons and new baby needed their mother.

A couple days after the delivery her OB-GYN shared that he was so relieved that both of them were doing well as it was hit or miss throughout her time in the hospital. God is good and I have learned that He's always good even when things don't turn out the way I desire.

On the day Ami was discharged, I strapped Haidyn in and helped Ami into the passenger seat. I got in, turned the key and flipped on the radio. Guess which song was playing? "Can't Live a Day Without You." We sat and cried, praising Him for His goodness. I thanked Him for being with us and allowing me to have my wife and daughter with me.

Would I have liked to stay and coach a potential regional and state champion? Absolutely! But the decision was easy; my marriage, wife and family came before anything but God. He has brought us through it all!

God has been calling me to disciple others in His Love and Lordship. He has encouraged and equipped me to teach others to seek Christ as Lord and to walk as His disciples, building up Godly men and marriages, and faithful husbands, fathers and families. He continues to confirm the calling.

Through the years of learning and growing, God has shaped and pruned me, and this message for His Kingdom purpose, and He continues to confirm the calling.

In this book I tell stories of men, women, marriages, and families whose lives the Love and Lordship of Christ have radically changed. They are all true but the names have been changed to protect the identity of the people involved.

My hope and prayer is that your knowledge of the Bible and personal relationship with Jesus will grow exponentially after reading this book.

SECTION 1

AUTHORITY

&

LOVE

CHAPTER 1

TRUE AUTHORITY

"My determination is to be my utmost for His Highest. ***To get there is a question of will, not of debate nor of reasoning, but a surrender of will, an absolute and irrevocable surrender on that point.*** *An overweening consideration for ourselves is the thing that keeps us from that decision, though we put it that we are considering others. When we consider what it will cost others if we obey the call of Jesus, we tell God He does not know what our obedience will mean. Keep to the point; He does know. Shut out every other consideration and keep yourself before God for this one thing only – My Utmost for His Highest. I am determined to be absolutely and entirely for Him and for Him alone."*

— Oswald Chambers, *My Utmost for His Highest*

(emphasis added)

How does Christ's Love affect our relationship with Him and others? How does His Authority or Lordship in our life impact our relationships? Are we living according to His Love and in His Lordship?

For our purpose, authority and lordship are synonymous and leadership flows from who or whatever is the authority or lord in your life.

Authority & Love – A Real Life Story

Dennis came in late one afternoon and sat down in my office. It was a few days before Christmas and the days were getting shorter and the burdens heavier.

He told me he thought his marriage was over. He'd tried to be a servant-leader to his new wife and blended family, but nothing seemed to work. So he'd reverted to demanding, yelling, foul language after she had pushed all his buttons and called him a few choice names.

I asked him why he chose to enter into the shouting match and "control game." He simply said, "It's all I've ever known, all I've ever seen. When things get bad, you just buck up and take control."

Sound familiar? It is one of the most common themes I see in couples and marriages. Love is lived out as feelings and emotions and when they get out of control, there is little love and a lot of accusations, demands and "lording it over."

God, in His Word, has much to say about authority and love and both are necessary to build Godly relationships.

With that said, I want to make sure we're all speaking the same language as you make your way through this book.

I don't know about you but I probably should have paid a bit more attention in English class. It's important to recognize and understand "root words" that give us insight into a word's meaning. If we don't know the root word, then we are either already lost and/or easily deceived.

Authority & The Author

As we focus on authority, we will see that in God's Kingdom Love and Lordship can never be separated.

Everybody knows that lordship is authority or control and love is a feeling, right? Unfortunately, these fallacies persist in our culture. Maybe that's the problem and why we need to better understand Authority.

What do you think of when you hear "authority?"

When I'm sharing this message, in particular in prisons and addiction rehab facilities, the first answer is almost always, "police," followed by "courts, government," and "boss, manager and superior." You get the picture.

While authority may connote these ideas, we need to begin with the root word to truly understand what authority is.

Author is the root word of "authority." This means that before we define authority as controlling or ruling over someone by position or rank, we need to understand who the "author" is for that rank, position, or title. Knowing the Author means we can define and determine what everything else is according to the Author's Truth.

It's this simple. The Author is God, The Father, Son, and Holy Spirit, and He has revealed Himself to us in His Word, The Bible. This means that Authority comes from Him and is what He says it is.

Now you can choose to believe He is not the Authority, but if you do that then who will be the authority in your life? Whoever is the strongest, has the most money, the most power or control? Yourself?

Now we begin to see how authority gets aligned with control and ruling or lording over others as it is rooted in selfishness and control. If I don't like your position and the way you do things, then I simply need to accumulate enough money, followers or power, and I can overthrow you and make the rules myself.

The battle for worldly authority is never good and never settled.

So we need an Author to truly have Authority, and we need to know what the Author says. Why Love and Lordship? Because I've learned in my own life and in being married, raising children, coaching and teaching young people, and mentoring men and couples, that even in our churches, these are two of the most used and talked about words— yet very few in our culture and world today know what they really are.

You know who does? The Author! Why not look at what He says about Love and Lordship so we can be grounded and rooted in True Authority.

God & Christ as The Author

If God is the Author (and He is), then we should submit to Him as the Authority. This means that His Word is Truth and His Truth is lived out in the Order (principles and priorities) that He authored or designed. It also means that we must do this in every part of our lives— individually, relationally, collectively/communally, and systemically. God's divine order always moves in this pattern.

God's design is that we only can go as far as "leadership" will take us and in the direction that "leaders" are going. Are we following God's design or is it evident that we are not raising up godly leaders—in marriage and family, in our churches, and in our world?

If we are living according to God's plan and Word, then we will be encouraged to stand strong and keep the faith. If, however, we are not following His plan and Word—and culture would seem to reveal this to be the case—then our conviction will challenge us to humbly accept and change what we are doing for our sake, and for the sake of His Family and Kingdom.

Here are Scriptures regarding God's Authority placed in Christ...

In **Matthew 28:18** Jesus said, "All authority has been given to me." By whom? The answer is: God the Father gave it to him. Keep reading...

Matthew 11:27 "All things have been handed over to me by my Father, and no one knows the Son except the Father, and no one knows the Father except the Son and anyone to whom the Son chooses to reveal him."

John 3:35 "The Father loves the Son and has given all things into his hand."

John 13:3, 5 "Jesus, knowing that the Father had given all things into his hands, and that he had come from God and was going back to God...began to wash the apostles' feet."

Ephesians 1:20–21 "God raised him from the dead and seated him at his right hand in the heavenly places, far above all rule and authority and power and dominion, and every name that is named, not only in this age but also in the one to come."

John 17:2 "Father, the hour has come; glorify your Son that the Son may glorify you, for you granted him authority over all flesh, to give eternal life to all whom you have given him."

Philippians 2:9-11 "Therefore God exalted him to the highest place and gave him the name that is above every name that at the name of Jesus every knee should bow, in heaven and on earth and under the earth, and every tongue acknowledge that Jesus Christ is Lord, to the glory of God the Father."

CHAPTER 2

BUT WHY AUTHORITY?
LET'S JUST LOVE ONE ANOTHER

Why authority? Authority affects everything, whenever and however it is rightly or wrongly expressed.

Authority is lordship. Authority is leadership. But what if we're doing it all wrong? What if we, as human beings, expressing our true human nature, lean toward authority as control, demanding, results-oriented only?

As Christ followers we are taught that authority is different—completely different. As a matter of fact, authority, according to Christ, and God's Word, is totally upside-down from what we think it is, or maybe what we would like it to be.

You say, "Oh, I know that authority is humbly serving others." But do we? As I look at the way most people are taught to lead—in their vocation, church, home, or even in positions of power—there seems to be a very familiar pattern.

That pattern looks a lot like the 12 apostles Jesus picked who wrestled to sit on the throne in His kingdom. If it showed up in Jesus' handpicked disciples how much more likely are we to struggle with authority?

Many modern churches compare their teaching to the world's standards and claim to be sharing God's Truth. The only standard to be held up as God's Truth is His Word and we would do well to teach all of it!

Authority is Lordship & Leadership

In Scripture God has some very specific things to say about authority and lordship, but unfortunately we tend to overlook, ignore, or redefine it with what works best for us. In so doing, we are almost always upside-down and missing what True Authority looks like and how we are to model and honor it.

The first and greatest command speaks to God's Authority, but it is often overlooked because "love," at least in our worldly definition, is so much more pleasant to talk about. Look at what Jesus had to say when He was asked which was the most important command.

Mark 12:29-31 begins with, **"The most important one,"** answered **Jesus, "is this: 'Hear, O Israel: The Lord our God, the Lord is one.** Love the Lord your God with all your heart and with all your soul and with all your mind and with all your strength.' The second is this: 'Love your neighbor as yourself.' There is no commandment greater than these." (Emphasis added)

Before Jesus talks about love and its importance, He echoes what God told Moses in Deuteronomy 6:4-5. He states that God is alone, The One and Only, worthy of all our praise and worship. Every person hearing Moses, and Jesus, say these words would have understood that the priority command begins with recognizing and honoring God as Lord, as The Author, The One with All Authority. Everything else flows from this first and most important command.

Jesus reinforced this before He left earth the first time in what we refer to as the Great Commission found in Matthew 28:18: "Then Jesus came to them and said, 'All authority in heaven and on earth has been given to me.'"

If we do not understand and accept that God is The One True Authority then nothing else lines up. We can define love and everything else the way we want. We can call the shots but will only have the appearance of being in control. And that's exactly what happens when we ignore The Author and His Truth.

Beginning with the Author impacts how we love, build relationships—especially marriage and family—and how we grow His Church and advance His Kingdom to influence the world and culture.

In order to have real leadership (authority), we should begin where God's Word begins: All Authority begins and ends with Christ. We seek leadership in our communities, state, and nation, in our businesses, schools, media, and churches. Yet Scripture teaches only two places where authority—headship or leadership—is to be developed: the Home (Ephesians 5:21-33) and the Church (Christ's Family), and leadership is to follow that order (1 Timothy 3:4-5).

Far too often we see so-called 'leaders' who wield the sword and scepter rather than truly serve pushing for power and influence at the expense of serving and 'leading' their marriage and family. This has led to a dearth of true authority and leadership in our communities and country.

Teaching True Authority

There is a great temptation in our broken and fallen humanity to want to 'rule or lord over' others. Real leadership comes from a humble, submissive, servant heart, not selfish ambition disguised by false humility and fleshly service to make a name, achieve a position, or gain wealth or status. Christ's teaching is very clear: those who truly lead are those who humbly place others above themselves and serve without expecting anything in return.

In Matthew 20:20-24, the 12 handpicked, cream-of-the-crop apostles begin to argue over who should sit on the thrones (seats of authority) when Christ entered His Kingdom. After all, isn't that what they'd signed up for—to rule and reign with the King of kings and Lord of lords?

James and John had sent their mommy to ask Jesus if they could occupy the prime seats in His Kingdom. When the other ten heard about it, the Bible says, "they were moved with indignation against the two brothers." If these were the best that Jesus could find, then there's hope for all of us! Jesus knew that, while they were unlearned and prideful, they were teachable.

And that's just what Jesus did. He taught them about real authority.

"Jesus called them together and said, 'You know that the rulers of the Gentiles lord it over them, and their high officials exercise authority over them. Not so with you. Instead, whoever wants to become great among you must be your servant, and whoever wants to be first must be your slave—just as the Son of Man did not come to be served, but to serve, and to give his life as a ransom for many.'" (Matthew 20:25-28)

Some translations insert the word "unbelievers" or "sinners" for Gentiles. That's how sinners define and exercise authority. It should not be so with those who believe. Jesus was the ultimate example of real authority or lordship.

There is a great temptation to want to 'rule or lord over' others. Christ's teaching is very clear: those who truly lead are those who humbly place others above themselves and serve without expecting anything in return.

The Essence of True Authority

"Jesus knew that the Father had put all things under his power, and that he had come from God and was returning to God." (John 13:3)

"For by the grace given me I say to every one of you: Do not think of yourself more highly than you ought, but rather think of yourself with sober judgment, in accordance with the faith God has distributed to each of you." (Romans 12:3)

"For we are God's handiwork, created in Christ Jesus to do good works, which God prepared in advance for us to do." (Ephesians 2:10)

Knowing who we are in Christ is at the heart of understanding True Authority. He modeled it in His own life and asks us to do the same. Knowing who we are recreated (He changes us or makes us new) to be in Him allows us to serve without consideration for what others think, or how the world ranks or rates us. We simply serve out of love and humility, confident and content in who we are so we can raise others above ourselves as we serve them. This is the essence of True Authority!

Modeling True Authority

"When he had finished washing their feet, he put on his clothes and returned to his place. "Do you understand what I have done for you?" he asked them. "You call me 'Teacher' and 'Lord,' and rightly so, for that is what I am. Now that I, your Lord and Teacher, have washed your feet, you also should wash one another's feet. I have set you an example that you should do as I have done for you. Very truly I tell you, no servant is greater than his master, nor is a messenger greater than the one who sent him. Now that you know these things, you will be blessed if you do them." (John 13:12-17)

Jesus taught and modeled very clearly that any authority in our lives it is to be exercised through our humble love and service to others. We are blessed as we follow His example.

CHAPTER 3

AUTHORITY ACCORDING TO GOD'S COVENANT ORDER

True Authority in The Home

"For the husband is the head of the wife as Christ is the head of the church, his body, of which he is the Savior." (Ephesians 5:23)

"Wives, submit yourselves to your own husbands as you do to the Lord." (Ephesians 5:22)

"Submit to one another out of reverence for Christ." (Ephesians 5:21)

The place where the true authority from Christ begins is in the most intimate of relationships—marriage, family and the home. No wonder the enemy relentlessly attacks the home above all else. He must know that if he can destroy marriage, family, and the home, then he can cripple and/or destroy everything else. Husbands, before we ever claim any authority in our marriage and with our wives, and wives before we try to feign any submission toward our husbands, we should note Christ's example (John 13:1-17) and heed the verse above: "Submit to one another out of reverence for Christ."

True Authority in Christ's Church

"Here is a trustworthy saying: Whoever aspires to be an elder desires a noble task. Now the overseer is to be above reproach, faithful to his wife, temperate, self-controlled, respectable, hospitable, able to teach, not given to drunkenness, not violent but gentle, not quarrelsome, not a lover of money. He must manage his own family well and see that his children obey him, and he must do so in a manner worthy of full respect. (If anyone does not know how to manage his own family, how can he take care of God's church?) He must not be a recent convert, or he may become conceited and fall under the same judgment as the devil. He must also have a good reputation with outsiders, so that he will not fall into disgrace and into the devil's trap." (2 Timothy 3:1–7)

Other than 'headship' in the Home, this explanation of authority in Christ's Church is the only other clearly defined outline for relational leadership in Scripture. The qualities of a True Leader (elder/overseer hinge on five key elements:

1) Godly character and integrity;

2) Ability to teach and shepherd others;

3) Servant-leader in the marriage and family (absence of this clearly negates leadership in His Church);

4) Humble maturity in the faith and;

5) A good reputation in the community.

God is showing us true authority and the priority of relationships from which it is to be learned, modeled, and lived out. Character is developed in marriage and family, wisdom is honed, and the humility that comes from wisdom (James 3:13) is derived. The home is also where every other area of leadership is to come from, including and especially in His Church. The Author tells us that when we miss it in our homes we will struggle to find it in Christ's Church or anywhere else.

True Authority in The World

"Jabez was more honorable than his brothers... Jabez cried out to the God of Israel, 'Oh, that you would bless me and enlarge my territory! Let your hand be with me, and keep me from harm so that I will be free from pain.' And God granted his request." (1 Chronicles 4:9a-10)

Known as the "Prayer of Jabez" this passage carries a great deal of insight, not the least of which is the simple fact that Jabez's honor (character) was instrumental to God's granting the "enlargement of his territory," literally "greater influence." Character and servant-leadership (true authority) go hand-in-hand in Scripture with 'leaders' defined almost exclusively in the Home and Church. God wanted us to learn how to truly lead (serve) in the settings and relationships where the most is at stake.

President John Adams, one of the founding fathers, stated, "Public virtue cannot exist in a nation without private, and public virtue is the only foundation of republics." We have sought our leaders, even in churches (public virtue), from those who've simply had success in the corporate, financial, or other realms. Often this was at the sacrifice of the personal life, the home, marriage, and family (private virtue). Maybe we should heed God's Word and seek our leaders from our marriages, families, homes, and from Christ's Church!

The Rest of The Story

I asked Dennis how leading the way he'd always known had worked for him?

This tough, blue-collar guy looked up with tears in his eyes and said, "It never has and it's not now." After a long pause, he said, "I really love my wife and want this marriage to work and I don't think it's going to."

"Then let's try something different," I said. We started looking first at the connection between true authority and real love.

In God's Kingdom True Authority is not about control, it's about serving. It's not about demanding, it's about giving. It's not about being first, it's about stepping to the back of the line and trusting The Lord. Why? Because real authority, at its heart, is not about persuading others to your point of view. It's about inviting them to Him and them inviting you to share more of Him and His Love and Lordship with them! In other words, authority, according to The Author's teaching and modeling is invited influence.

I saw Dennis and his wife some time later and both had smiles on their faces. As they walked past me, he smiled and nodded as if to say, "God's way is much better than mine."

God's Word boldly establishes that He (Father, Son, and Holy Spirit) is The Author and, therefore, the One True Authority! His Word (Living in Christ and written in The Bible) tells us plainly that if we have seen (know) Jesus, then we have seen (know) The Father. (John 14:8-10)

We've laid the foundation of True Authority/Lordship and relational servant-leadership. We'll look next at what it means for Christ to be Lord.

In our flesh and in our culture, just as with the apostles, we desire and are told that authority is about being in control. It's about demanding the most influence and keeping everything and everyone "under your thumb."

Why is Christ's the only True Authority and why is His Lordship so important? Because as Oswald Chambers tells us using the example of Paul's life, "The mainspring of Paul's service is not love for men, but love for Jesus Christ. If we are devoted to the cause of humanity, we shall soon be crushed and broken-hearted for we shall often meet with more ingratitude from men than we would from a dog; but if our motive is love to God, no ingratitude can hinder us from serving our fellow man."

We can only do this in Christ's Love and only when He is our Lord, our True Authority.

STUDY GUIDE
AUTHORITY & LOVE

Key Concepts

1) True Authority comes from God (Father, Son and Holy Spirit), The Author.

2) The world/culture defines and practices authority as control or lording over others, emphasizing results over people.

3) God defines/models in Christ, relational servant-leadership as authority.

4) Authority as relational servant-leadership begins in the marriage and family.

5) Authority in Christ's Church is to be an extension of good leadership in the home.

6) True Authority prioritizes people and relationships over things, outcomes and success.

Discussion Questions

1) How have you seen authority practiced or modeled in your life, family, church or vocation?

2) How have you practiced authority?

3) What do you think motivates us to practice authority as Gentiles, unbelievers or sinners?

4) What steps will you identify and take to practice authority as Christ taught and modeled it?

5) How does the last quote in this chapter by Oswald Chambers make you think differently about Christ's love and lordship, and how you are to follow Him?

6) Would your home be different if you modeled relational servant-leadership? Your church? Your workplace?

SECTION 2

THE STORY OF TWO KINGDOMS

CHAPTER 4

THE KINGDOM & LORDSHIP OF CHRIST

"Temptation usually comes through a door that's been deliberately left open."

— Scottish Theologian Arnold Glasgow

John came up to me after a Sunday morning church service and asked if I remembered him. "Of course," I said.

"Can we meet? I'm struggling and I understand that you work with men and couples in difficult relationships."

"We sure can." I looked at my calendar and we found a time to meet. Then I asked, "How can I pray specifically for you?"

He shared, "My first marriage is over and I'm losing my two children as well. I can't let that happen and I need help."

That exchange led to a year of weekly mentoring and discipleship. John explained that while he provided well for his wife and children, he'd chosen his own lifestyle in his first marriage.

John's passions and desires were not unlike those of many young married men with two little children in the house. He wasn't getting enough attention (read sex) so he found it wherever he could—bars, strip clubs, business trips.

His wife had enough and filed for divorce. It went from bad to worse as John continued to seek his own desires, and now it was going to cost him his children.

That's where The Lord began to get his attention. But old habits die hard, especially the ones that bring us the most immediate reward. Sexual sin is one of the easiest to fall into and the most difficult to conquer and be freed from.

He knew The Lord but had decided, like so many others, that he was doing fine as he continued to live as he desired, show up at church, give a little money, and convinced himself that all was well. After all, the reason we had connected was because he was dating a lady that went to our church and that was going pretty well.

About four months into our weekly discipleship we found ourselves in a deep conversation about lust, pornography and sexual sin. He abruptly got up from the table and told me he'd explain his sudden departure the next week in person.

I wished him well and prayed for him as he hurried out the door. The following Thursday he came bounding into the restaurant with a big smile on his face. You'll read the story he told me a little later in this section.

John was living much the same as many others in our culture. Even if they attend church, it's usually not so much to know Jesus but to assuage their conscience, and/or keep up appearances. Or maybe it's because their girlfriend, boyfriend or spouse, even their extramarital "partner" goes to church. However, their lives do not reflect that Christ is Lord. Their hearts do not fully belong to Him.

The fictional Father Smith sums up how many live their lives apart from God unknowingly seeking Him, "The man who rings the bell at the brothel, unconsciously does so seeking God." (Bruce Marshall, The World, The Flesh and Father Smith.)

We could substitute various options for "brothel." We fill the emptiness with drugs, drink, food, marriage, spouse, children, family, on and on—even "church." Many of these only destroy lives, several are noble and worthy, but none should supersede Christ in our lives.

Augustine said it this way: "Thou hast made us for thyself, O Lord, and our heart is restless until it finds its rest in thee."

Christ as Lord

In Section 1 we discussed that God as Father, Son, and Holy Spirit is the Authority and we need to look to Him, in particular to Christ, as The Father has placed all Authority in His hands.

"Then Jesus came to them and said, 'All authority in heaven and on earth has been given to me.'" (Matthew 28:18)

"Jesus knew that the Father had put all things under his power, and that he had come from God and was returning to God." (John 13:3)

Our natural selfish desires with regard to authority always incline us toward demanding respect, control, attention and results. Jesus contrasted this with Godly Authority—being last instead of first, serving instead of being served, placing others above self.

As John's story tells us, old habits die hard. It is difficult to let go of control, especially once we've gotten it and made it work for us. But that literally means we are playing "lord" in our lives rather than submitting to Christ.

So, what's the big deal, you say? I'm a good person, attend church, don't kill or abuse animals and help needy people once in a while.

That's nice, but you do see that you're justifying "lordship" of your own life against the standards of the world, all while feigning Christ as Lord?

Whenever someone comes to see me about struggles or problems in their life—marriage and family or otherwise—I begin with the following chart to find out where their heart is.

Lordship (Authority)
⬇
Discipleship
⬇
Relationship
⬇
Sin/Addictions/Issues

I then follow up with this statement that sums up the first step toward a solution to every person's or couples' problems: "All of the issues we will discuss today, and moving forward, stem from the first two, but so often we only deal with the symptoms that occur in the latter two."

Lordship is of Utmost Importance

For some, the root issues become apparent right away. Yet often, as with John, we have to dig deeper to find what is really being fed or protected before the person will truly admit that they are trying to run their own life. The enemy's greatest deception is, "You can be master of your own fate; you don't need a lord." He's simply appealing to our natural desire to be in authority, in control.

At this point I ask: "How's that been working for you?"

Usually the light begins to flicker. Now we can talk about why it is of utmost importance that Christ is Lord of our lives and the evidence, no matter how much we want to think otherwise, is that we have not made Him so.

By luring us away from The Author, Satan gets us to define words and concepts according to our whims and desires rather than according to God's Truth.

Dr. Gary Chapman, author of Five Love Languages, states, "Love is the most important word in the English language—and the most confusing."

When I ask couples or conference attendees to define "love," we have nearly as many definitions as we do people. Why is that? Because we've fallen for the lie that "love" is whatever we want it to be in making us feel good and fulfilled. It's all rooted in feelings and satisfaction in the moment.

We have chosen to redefine terms relatively, again falling for Satan's deception to lure us from God's Authority and Truth.

Paraphrasing NASA, "Church, we have a problem!"

CHAPTER 5

AUTHORITY & TRUTH

We all need a solid foundation and it must reflect the authority on which we base our decisions and build our lives and relationships. The foundation, good or bad, is rooted in lordship and discipleship. Who are you a disciple of—Christ as Lord or the enemy as lord?

Lordship and discipleship reveal everything about your life and what you believe. Regardless of what you say to anyone, the choices you make daily in church, at the office, or anywhere else, reveal that you have a lord and you are someone's disciple.

Let me share with you how we help people begin to understand this universal principle and, even more importantly, recognize how it is playing out in their lives. If we don't have an absolute foundation of Truth then words and their application can mean what anyone wants them to mean. What happens when the inevitable conflict occurs? Everything crumbles if we don't have Truth.

The following five words and contrasting definitions are not all-inclusive, but they are integral and help us cover a lot of ground in getting people to see where they truly live their lives.

Contrasting Language for God's Truth & The World

WORD	WORLD	TRUTH
Love	'If it feels good, do it'	Commitment
Humility	Humiliation	True Confidence
Authority	Dictate, control, 'lord over'	Lead by example
Integrity	Reputation over Character	Shalom, integer
Discipleship	No "lord" needed	Student-servant

With this chart we can begin to ask questions, discuss how decisions are made, and ask people to share the truth their answers reveal about who or what is Lord or lord in their life.

No one questions the worldly definitions; we've all lived them. Remember, "for all have sinned and fall short of the glory of God." (Romans 3:23)

Below, we apply Scripture defining each "TRUTH" in contrast to worldly concepts, laying the foundation for determining who is truly our Lord or lord and the impact on our lives.

1) Love as Commitment – The Truth lies in Christ and The Cross as the greatest example of Love ever given. Matthew 26:53, "Do you think I cannot call on my Father, and he will at once put at my disposal more than twelve legions of angels?" With this statement, Jesus tells us He had a choice and that none of it felt good. Think about how Jesus felt relationally as His best friends all abandoned Him. (Matthew 26:56) How do you think He felt socially with the crowds crying, "Crucify Him!"? (Matthew 27:22-23)

What about mentally and emotionally as He was in so much anguish in the garden that He sweated drops of blood? (Luke 22:44)

Obviously He did not feel good physically as He was mocked, spit on, flogged, beaten, and crucified. (Matthew 26:67-68; 27; 26-31; Luke 23:33-34; John 19:1-17)

One final thought on love and feelings: How do you think He felt spiritually as He cried out, "My God, My God, why have you forsaken me?" (Mark 15:34)

Think about it, if love were a feeling, what would Jesus have done? He would have looked to His Father and said, "Nope, this feels awful and if 'love' is a feeling, this must not be love at all. I'm outta here!"

Instead, the Truth is that love is a commitment. He loved His Father and us, so He remained committed and obedient (in love) to His Father and for us to show what love truly is. "Father, forgive them for they do not know what they are doing." (Luke 23:34)

We must understand that Jesus here is modeling the greatest commands for us. In Luke 22:42, He petitions the Father, asking if He could be spared from the cup of suffering and sacrifice. Obviously, the answer was "no" (a great lesson that God always answers our prayers but not always as we want) as Jesus then continued to submit to and fulfill The Father's plan. He is obedient in following through to the Cross, showing His first and highest love was to His Father (Mark 12:30). As He then completed God's plan in dying on the

Cross, He gave His life in an ultimate act of love (John 15:13) for all who would believe in Him—you and me—loving others as He loved Himself (Mark 12:31).

Love is a choice, a commitment, an act of the will for the sake of others, according to The Author's words and example.

2) Humility as True Confidence and Contentment – I once read a Tweet from a prominent author and pastor that said, "Humility is not thinking less of yourself, it's not thinking of yourself at all," echoing a very common misconception about humility.

Matthew 22:39 states, "Love your neighbor as you love yourself." Romans 12:3 says, "Do not think of yourself more highly than you should but think of yourself with sober judgment according to the measure of faith God has given you." And finally, Jesus Himself modeled this kind of humility and love in John 13:3, "Jesus knew that the Father had put all things under his power, and that he had come from God and was returning to God."

According to God's Word and Christ's example, humility is knowing who you are in Christ so you can choose to place others above yourself. God knew that unless we are confident and content in who we are, attempts to put others above self would end in "false humility" or pride.

3) Authority was explained in Chapter 1 with the clear contrast of the disciples and the world desiring to control or "lord over" others in Christ's Kingdom (Matthew 20:20-24) and Christ teaching them serving as real authority (vv. 25-28).

4) Integrity is another term that has been watered down by placing success and reputation above character. Hall of Fame Coach John Wooden said, "Be more concerned with your character than your reputation, because your character is what you really are, while your reputation is merely what others think you are." There are numerous examples in our culture where people propped themselves up with success and an outward reputation only to see it all crumble. Think Enron, Firestone and Worldcom in the early 2000s to name a few.

Integrity according to God's word is very closely related to the Greek word for integer or akéraios, which means whole, integral or undivided. If you remember your second grade math lessons, you'll know that an integer is a "whole number." Integrity is also found in the Hebrew word, "Shalom" which is most often interpreted as "peace."

So what do whole numbers have to do with peace and integrity? I'm glad you asked.

Shalom actually has at least 27 meanings in English. The closest words to capturing the full meaning of Shalom are "completeness" or "wholeness." Integrity or akeraiótita, from the same root word as integer or whole number, literally means uprightness and is found in wholeness. We find Shalom or peace when we apply the whole of God's Truth to every part of our lives. This is the character of integrity, not the world's compromise of reputation sufficing for character.

5) Finally, we come to discipleship. This is crucial to understanding Lordship as it defines our response to the Lord or lord in our life. Just as profound is our understanding of the enemy's use of this in our lives. We will build on discipleship in Section Three.

CHAPTER 6

THE FALSE KINGDOM

The Serpent's Deception: You Can Be Lord of Your Own Life

Satan knew that God had given us free choice and that is where he got mankind to fall. It's still the source of every sin today. Satan can't stand God and tries desperately to dethrone Him—but he can't. Yet God has given him an eternal kingdom that completely contrasts Christ's Kingdom. So, Satan does all that he can to get us to believe that we don't need a lord, which means we don't need to be a disciple to anyone. This is the root of The Fall and Sin.

In direct contrast, Christ is calling us to be His disciples and make disciples for Him. Jesus calls us to be His "student-servants" (to learn from Him and emulate Him). If we are His disciples, that is what we will do. If we are not, then we have another lord and are someone else's disciples. Don't fall for Satan's lie; you are a disciple to someone. You need to know who that is and what that looks like.

Prayerfully apply the chart, terms and related Scriptures from the previous chapter in your own life. Ask The Spirit to show you where you are when it comes to His Truth, Authority, and Lordship.

Satan's Greatest & Only Deception

You've likely heard many sermons or messages on the serpent's lies and deception to lure Eve and Adam into sin and The Fall.

All of this is true but I want to focus on something I think is much more alluring and therefore destructive in Satan's scheme. He not only used it as the final and fatal appeal with Adam and Eve, but he continues to do so today.

Take a look at the Genesis 3 interaction between the serpent and Eve: "Now the serpent was more crafty than any of the wild animals the LORD God had made. He said to the woman, "Did God really say, 'You must not eat from any tree in the garden'?"

Two things to consider here for our own walk with Christ as Lord:

1) Rephrase this and ask yourself, "Do you really know God's Truth?" That's what he wants to know. Are you spending time to know His Truth or can the enemy confuse you with the same question?

2) The serpent cunningly asked if God had restricted them from eating from any of the trees. He didn't just focus on the one God had forbidden as he wanted to see if Eve truly knew the Truth of what God had said. How easily we can be deceived if we do not spend time in His Word to seek and know His Truth.

"We may eat of the fruit of the trees of the garden: But of the fruit of the tree which is in the midst of the garden, God hath said, You shall not eat of it, neither shall you touch it, lest you die." (vv. 2-3 NKJV)

Eve's reply reveals her incomplete knowledge of God's Absolute Truth. The question and her partial knowledge accomplished two things the serpent desired: Partial truth led to her confusion and; her response literally "created" an alternate or relative "truth" that likely worked in her favor.

Now we have "two truths," God's (don't eat) and Eve's (don't touch). What to do? Relativism is as old as human nature and the enemy used that very human nature and the free will necessary for love to confuse and deceive. Don't fall for the lies. God's Absolute Truth can never be compromised.

"And the serpent said unto the woman, you shall not surely die." (v. 4 NKJV) The serpent calls God a liar, he appeals to Eve's desire to live and disputes God's Words, yet Eve still has not given in. The serpent is laying the groundwork for his grand finale and the source of every sin since, including yours and mine.

"For God knows that when you eat from it your eyes will be opened, and **you will be like God, knowing good and evil.**" (v. 5, emphasis added) Ah! The coup de grâce that continues to appeal to every human being that has ever existed.

CHAPTER 7

ONLY TWO KINGDOMS, TWO KINGS, TWO LORDS

The Serpent (Satan) Springs the Trap

Track with me here as we see the serpent build on the confusion and, I beleive, desire coming from the free will that God had given to Adam and Eve to accomplish his ultimate goal: death or seperation from God. He springs the final trap and secures his prey. He does this in two strokes that we all struggle with:

1) He uses a lie to appeal to Eve's free will. The lie is: "Guess what? You don't need a God or Lord; you can be lord of your own kingdom and life!" Brilliant! He knows that free will desires to be in control and he offers a fake kingdom—our own.

    He doesn't care that it's a lie. He knows that when we reject Christ and live out our own lives in our own kingdoms we've chosen the only other kingdom: Satan's. This is tough to swallow, but it's true and we need to understand it.

2) He finishes the deception by presenting relativism to Eve (and to us): "You will know good and evil." How awesome is this? The Hebrew word here for "know" includes, and is probably best translated as, "classify." In one fell swoop the enemy presents us with our own non-existent kingdom where we can make up our own rules and laws. Sound familiar?

It's this simple: there are only two kingdoms, which means there are only two Kings, two Lords. There are only God's and Christ's Kingdom of Light and Life, and Satan's kingdom of death and darkness. So don't fall for the lie that you can be king or lord, "be like God."

The bottom line: We can and must know to which Kingdom we belong. Don't be deceived. Know Christ as Lord and know His Truth. He came and died for you to make that possible.

Deception & Relativism – Consent Replaces Covenant

I present the Love & Lordship series multiple times annually at prisons, residential addiction rehab facilities, and to men's groups where many are ordered to attend by the court or government. After the first couple of sessions on Lordship and Discipleship, we dive into relationships.

When I get to the discussion on lust and porneia I often refer back to the original deception of Eve in the Garden by the serpent and equate it to how we redefine sexuality and sex to accommodate our own desires. I discuss how we create our own convenient "truths" to support what we want. I ask the men if they have ever stolen anything and for years 100% of the hands went up.

On one particular day, three guys said they had not taken or stolen anything. I asked if they had ever taken any girl's virginity or virtue and they all said, "Oh, yeah." Immediately two of them then said, "But they willingly gave it."

The Holy Spirit instantly laid this on my heart: "Oh, so you consented and she consented, but God never consented. His Truth didn't change."

You could hear a pin drop! Isn't that how we choose the tree of knowledge of good and evil? We justify and rationalize our own truth for our own pleasure. We ignore His Truth when it doesn't fit what we want, but we will still have to answer to His Word and will.

Consent (our "truth") is a bad substitute for covenant and commitment (God's Truth). This is an example of falling for Satan's lie that we can "be like God" and have our own kingdom that ultimately destroys many lives.

Path to Sin & The Fall

For practical purposes, check out the path below found in the serpent's temptation that led to Sin and The Fall of Adam and Eve and persists in our sins today. Think about how this applies to your life, temptations, sins, and struggles. Christ has made a way to rescue and redeem us.

1. **Confusion** – "Did God really say...?" Do I know His Truth?
2. **Deception** – "Surely you won't die." Do I fall for subtle lies?
3. **Touch** – "You must not touch it." Relativism leads to initial appeal to the flesh.
4. **Taste** – "Pleasing to the eye and desirable for gaining wisdom." Satisfy the flesh (senses and emotions rule rather than God's Truth).
5. **Indulge** – "She took some and ate it ... and he ate it." Please the senses (self).
6. **Addiction/Bondage** – "They realized they were naked... made coverings for themselves." Now caught in their sin they must cover it up.

28

Christ came to earth in the form of a baby in a manger for the express purpose of dying for our sins so that our relationship with God could be restored. His death on The Cross removed our sin(s) before God and made the way for us to live forever in His Kingdom. It's your choice.

Whoever is Lord in your life determines your every motive, thought, decision, action and relationship. Knowing Christ as Lord and His Truth makes all the difference when the subtle lies and temptations come from the enemy. It's a matter of life and death—and eternity!

In the world, authority is demanded, manipulated, and all about control and "lording it over" others, even when we do it nicely. In God's Kingdom, authority is invited influence in the lives of those who have willingly surrendered.

The Rest of the Story

When John arrived for our next weekly meeting, it was evident something had changed.

He shared with me that the previous week when we were discussing whether Christ was going to truly be Lord of his life and relationships, including his sex life, something clicked.

He said that as we discussed the sin of pornography/porneia (Greek word for sexual immorality or sexually immoral mindset and root word for pornography), lust and promiscuity, The Holy Spirit overwhelmed him. That's when he abruptly left. I'll let him tell you the rest of the story:

"I was planning to take my girlfriend from work the following day and spend the weekend at my lake house where we would consummate our wonderful 'Christian' relationship. The Holy Spirit made it clear that I couldn't follow through on that. I left the restaurant and, after spending some time in prayer, tears, and asking for forgiveness, I went straight to her office and asked her to come with me. She obliged and I took her to a quiet place and explained what we'd been talking about and that there was no way that we could go away for the weekend. In tears I asked for her forgiveness and she graciously gave it. From that day forward my life was changed."

John had rationalized that porn and sex as a divorced man and with other women were OK until God began to show him the consequences of his actions.

After dating a nice Christian lady for a few months that rationalization had changed. He was now committed and faithful to one person, so surely God understood that they were meant for each other and could

29

act upon that sexually prior to being married. He knew better, but the temptation was strong.

Choosing to be obedient to Christ as His Lord, John and his girlfriend chose to remain abstinent until they married six months later. He called me from their honeymoon to thank me and confirm that the sexual union of love in covenant was far better than any other he had ever experienced.

Just like John, we all have temptations rooted in our selfish fleshly desires that we know are wrong and pursue anyway, or justify and deceive ourselves in pursuit of them. Their end is destruction, as John found out. As he understood and began to walk with Jesus as Lord, everything changed.

Nearly 12 years later, John and his wife are now mentoring other couples to walk in The Lord.

What a beautiful blessing and reward to know your Lord! It will change everything for your good and His Glory. It's Discipleship and it's the only response that makes our lives worthwhile. Let's look further to find out what that entails.

"Never nourish an experience which has not God as its Source, and faith in God as its result. If you do, your experience is anti-Christian, no matter what visions you may have had. Is Jesus Christ Lord of your experiences, or do you try to lord it over Him? Is any experience dearer to you than your Lord? He must be Lord over you, and you must not pay attention to any experience over which He is not Lord. There comes a time when God will make you impatient with your own experience — 'I do not care what I experience; I am sure of Him.'"

— Oswald Chambers, *My Utmost for His Highest*

STUDY GUIDE
THE LORDSHIP OF CHRIST

Key Concepts

1) Whoever is your Lord/lord or authority defines your Truth/truth.

2) There are only two Kingdoms and therefore two Kings.

3) Truth is Absolute and the Foundation for all things.

4) Lordship is based on Absolute Truth and is inherent in all of life/relationships.

5) Your choices reveal the priorities in your life, reflecting who or what is in control of your life.

6) All sin in life comes from rebellion against His Lordship and failure to recognize and live in His Truth.

7) Christ's example shows us that authority is invited influence rather than demanding, manipulating or controlling.

8) Humility and Integrity are essential in all healthy lives and relationships.

Discussion Questions

1) Whoever is your Lord/lord or authority defines your Truth/truth.

2) There are only two Kingdoms and therefore two Kings.

3) Truth is Absolute and the Foundation for all things.

4) Lordship is based on Absolute Truth and is inherent in all of life/relationships.

5) Your choices reveal the priorities in your life, reflecting who or what is in control of your life.

6) All sin in life comes from rebellion against His Lordship and failure to recognize and live in His Truth.

7) Christ's example shows us that authority is invited influence rather than demanding, manipulating or controlling.

8) Humility and Integrity are essential in all healthy lives and relationships.

Lordship/Priorities Activity

1) On a piece of paper, make two columns with a margin in the middle. On the left make a list of the most important things in your life. What priorities have driven your life to this point? Be as brutally honest as you can.

2) On the right make a list of what you think or know your priorities should be according to God's Truth. One hint: Please don't put "church" at the top; begin with God/Christ. We'll learn more about this later.

3) Compare the lists.

If you're like most of us, you found the list on the left somewhat or completely out of line with the list on the right. Don't be discouraged. That's why Jesus came. But we need to be sure that He is Lord of our lives.

This exercise has helped many get a visual picture of what Lordship actually looks like, so as you follow through with the last step keep that in mind. It may seem odd at first, but stick with it. I pray you will begin to see what it means to make Christ Lord of your life.

4) Take your pen or pencil and remove "God/Christ" at the top of the list on the right. I know this is awkward, but trust me. Now in the margin of the list on the left write, "God/Christ" in front of the first item, no matter what it is. Repeat for every item on the left side.

Here's the point: You've likely tried everything you can to get rid of those things in your life that you know don't belong. The only way you can succeed is to make Christ Lord.

He alone has the power to remove the addictions, bad habits, sins, and struggles that persist in your life. Also you've probably been frustrated when those things that you know should be the most important have not received the priority. Again, Christ is the Only One Who has the power to re-order your life in line with His Truth and Love.

He has come to save us so we can be in a relationship with Him, and the only relationship we can be in with Him is if He is Lord. He will never force you to submit to Him. You have to willingly surrender. Only then can your life reflect His Lordship and line up with His Covenant Order and the blessings that come with it.

SECTION 3

DISCIPLESHIP: RESPONSE REQUIRED

*If Jesus Christ is King of kings
and Lord of lords and He is.
If Jesus Christ came to save all
who believe in Him so we could
be in a relationship with Him
and He did. If you have received
Him as Savior and claim to be
in that relationship with Him,
the only question that remains…
are you submitting to
Him as Lord of your life?*

CHAPTER 8

DISCIPLESHIP: RESPONDING TO YOUR LORD

Discipleship is Not Perfection, it's Lifelong Maturation

The ONLY WAY we can be in a relationship with Christ is with Him as Lord. We must be His disciple, or student-servant, with our whole heart and whole life set on Him. Wholehearted discipleship is not perfection, it is a lifelong maturation.

You are someone's disciple. Every part of your life reveals who is your Lord or lord.

When we talk of discipleship in this book it is based on the Scriptural principle of obedience-based discipleship, not simply knowledge-based learning, which is not really discipleship at all. Personal discipleship comes with the expectation of, and accountability for, obedience to His Word and in our walk with The Lord. Relational discipleship is training and holding others accountable to obedience as we share and apply His Word to make disciples.

A Discipleship Story

He came into my office, we prayed, and I looked up and he was weeping profusely. He'd already shared with me over the phone the reason for the tears so I asked him to fill me in as to how he and his now estranged wife had arrived at this painful point.

They had met in a Bible college and had been married nine years. He was sexually promiscuous before meeting her; she was not and they remained chaste in their courtship. He was "addicted" to porn, but as is often the case he kept it a tightly guarded secret.

With that dirty little "nugget" securely tucked away, they seemed to have had a really good relationship and sex life (according to him) the first four to five years. In time the guilt became too heavy and he confessed the porn to her. She practically cut him off from sex over the next four years. Though he tried to fight the temptation, he continued with porn and about three years after the confession he had an affair.

I shared with him that this was God's design coming true in the flesh: where the eyes and mind go the body will eventually follow.

She left him, and here he was sitting in my office having finally sought counsel as she had asked him to do years earlier after the initial porn confession. In pride, he had chosen not to.

He was heartbroken, full of guilt and shame, and missing his wife. She had made no contact with him in the four months since her departure.

He came into my office one week and said he was considering not continuing with any counseling, as it was doing no good. I asked what he meant and he said, "She's not coming back."

I asked. "What do you think you're here for?" He said, "To get my wife back and my marriage restored."

I responded, "If that happens, what's going to be different? You will still be the same prideful, lustful, sorry-for-yourself person. You're not here first and foremost to get her back and restore your marriage. You are here to understand what it means to be in a relationship with Christ and for Him to be Lord of your life—all of it! As you walk in this faithfully He will shape and mold you into His disciple and the man and husband that He died for and desires you to be. Then if your wife responds to His work and will in her life and comes back, you will be the husband and man that can make this marriage what God wants it to be. You're here to know Christ above all else."

He agreed with deeper sobs and more tears.

I tell that story for one simple reason. Here was a man and couple that met in Bible college, knew God's Word, and faithfully attended and served in their church. Yet secret sin was prevalent in his life that, once revealed, led to deeper sin and destructive consequences. The response from his wife, while certainly understandable, did not comport with God's Word. Now what God had put together, a man and woman had torn apart.

I'd like to say that the couple is back together and doing well but they are not as far as I know. The outcome is far from rare, although it is certainly a lesser occurrence in strong Bible-believing, Christ-centered homes and churches. The common denominator in most every story of broken covenant is that, like this church-attending, apparently happy-on-the-outside couple, many have never been discipled to be a disciple of Christ.

Our churches spend an inordinate amount of time and effort on marketing a message that attracts and keeps folks coming, making converts to their community. When it comes to making disciples of Jesus Christ in intimate loving relationships, there is a tremendous void.

This is a call to our homes and churches, especially those called to servant-leadership roles and responsibilities, to make His Lordship and our discipleship the overriding and all-consuming priority as His Word calls us to do!

Jesus on The Cost of Discipleship

We've already established that to be in a relationship with Jesus Christ means that He must be Lord and we must be His disciples. Let's explore what Our Lord Himself says about the cost of being His disciple.

It is nothing short of a tremendous gift of grace and blessing to be saved by Christ and to walk as His disciple. That does not mean that it is easy.

In Luke 14:25-35, Jesus describes the commitment (remember commitment is love) that is REQUIRED to be His disciple. Bear with me once again as I paraphrase for brevity and ask you to read the text yourself to determine whether or not I'm adhering to His stern call to discipleship.

As the crowds grew, Jesus' response was to ensure that they were following Him for the right reasons. (Compare this with many of today's churches, as we'll see this again later regarding John 6). His first comment was downright tough! Again this is my paraphrase so read it for yourself. Jesus says if anything in our life, including our own life, is more important than Him, then we can't be His disciples. He doesn't focus on money, fame, or stuff; He talks about the most important of relationships: marriage and family. Ouch! Anything in your life taking priority over Christ? This is a call to maturity in Christ. We may struggle and stumble, but His call is to determine and display in our hearts and lives that He is first and foremost.

He then describes the cost in two ways: 1) Financially – He describes someone attempting to build a tower that does so without considering what it will cost. The end result is a half-built tower and it becomes a focal point of ridicule for all who see it; 2) Battle – He describes a king going to battle with half the number of his enemy. Either he must determine whether he has a plan to defeat the enemy or he must come with a white flag and discuss "peace."

The outcome in the first example is that our life and what is produced by a weak faith is a mockery for those who witness it. In other words, Jesus is saying if you don't count the cost and sell out to Him, or live like He is first in your life, your faith is a laughingstock. We can't continue to display a faith that doesn't put Him first in all things.

In the Battle example, the result is a compromise and likely surrender. This is certainly not the victorious Christian life that His Word speaks of, as so many try to live with a partial or weak faith and claim they are His disciples. By His own words Jesus says that we can't be half-hearted and be His disciples.

OUCH AGAIN! And He's not finished yet.

Jesus goes on to say, "In the same way, those of you who do not give up everything you have cannot be my disciples." (Luke 14:33) How many of us are trying to be His disciples on our own compromised terms when, according to Him, we simply can't be and are not? What must He think of us?

Finally, He closes by stating that those who are trying to live as His disciples on their own terms essentially have no impact in His Kingdom. The impact of their saltiness is worthless.

Let me give you a final paraphrase in context with this passage that I pray will drive the point home and compel all those who call Him Savior to seek and desire to walk with Him as Lord. In essence Jesus is saying, if He's not first in our lives, if we do not count the cost of the calling and commitment, and we do not take up our own cross (i.e., go to the death of our own self and selfish desires) then we are not His disciples. Stated another way: If we are not willing to pay the price, then He is not our Lord and our faith is a mockery to those who observe us. Is it any wonder the culture is not drawn to our modern-day faith and to Christ but rather to our souped-up services designed to attract with little or no accountability and commitment expected? What does your discipleship response to Christ look like?

CHAPTER 9

DISCIPLESHIP: FINDING OUT WHO YOU WERE CREATED TO BE

Discipleship Requires Discipline

Discipleship is not only knowing Christ as Lord and exalting Him, it is allowing Him to reveal to us who we truly are in Him! As we make disciples we help others understand who they are in Christ and help them fulfill all He has created and called them to be—in life, relationships, community, and culture.

How then can we make discipleship not only a priority but also a reality? We turn to God's Word. I implore you to take to heart these four key principles and daily practice these disciplines to become His disciple and make disciples of others. Not one single principle will come naturally to you. That's why it's called discipleship; it requires the discipline of His indwelling Holy Spirit giving us the strength by faith to walk in His commands and overcome the selfish desires of our own natural, fleshly lusts:

1) Honorable Submission – "Submit to one another out of reverence for Christ." (Ephesians 5:21) Paul tells us that the key to every good relationship begins with our honor for Christ. In our reverence for Him we are then able to submit to others. Truly submitting to others was impossible for me until I learned to submit to Him. This is the essence of discipleship.

2) Honest Surrender – "Do not be deceived: God cannot be mocked. A man reaps what he sows. Who ever sows to please their flesh, from the flesh will reap destruction; whoever sows to please the Spirit, from the Spirit will reap eternal life. Let us not become weary in doing good, for at the proper time we will reap a harvest if we do not give up." (Galatians 6:7-9)

Look at Paul's instruction here for discipleship in Christ. First we must be brutally honest with ourselves: Deception is easy to do in my flesh. Over time His Spirit calls me away from this self-deception to integrity and honesty, which is impossible to do in my selfish flesh.

We can deceive ourselves, thinking we are Christ's disciples simply by attending church, giving some money, and serving from time to time. These are all good things and we need to do them, but they can be just actions of a fleshly heart seeking favor or attention from others rather than a heart truly surrendered to Christ.

The only way we can know and grow as His disciples is to honestly evaluate our motives, thoughts, and decisions to be sure they are surrendered to His Spirit and will. If we remain patient and persevere in this honest surrender, we will reap His harvest. That's discipleship.

3) Holy Sacrifice – "Therefore, I urge you, brothers and sisters, in view of God's mercy, to offer your bodies as a living sacrifice, holy and pleasing to God—this is your true and proper worship. Do not conform to the pattern of this world, but be transformed by the renewing of your mind. Then you will be able to test and approve what God's will is—his good, pleasing and perfect will. For by the grace given me I say to every one of you: Do not think of yourself more highly than you ought, but rather think of yourself with sober judgment, in accordance with the faith God has distributed to each of you." (Romans 12:1-3)

I suspect that many of you, like myself and many others I've shared this with, initially glossed over something incredibly important in this text.

It is clear that Paul, through the Holy Spirit, is calling us as disciples to sacrifice our life to God. What I so often missed was that this is not a salvation command, it is a post-salvation one. Paul is begging us to take what Christ has made "holy and pleasing to God" and surrender it back to God.

It is not our sacrifice that makes us holy and pleasing; it is His sacrifice that has already done that. Our job is to take what He has made right in God's eyes and faithfully and sacrificially return it to Him for His Glory. The difference from the Old Testament sacrifices is that we can choose to get up and walk away from the altar. Our sacrifice has to be of our own free will but, make no mistake, it is what we are called to.

He even tells us how we are to do this: Don't conform; instead, transform the way you think and act in line with God's Word.

He then encourages us with an assurance that if we will choose to be a Holy Sacrifice we will be living, walking proof of God's good and perfect will. But be careful, if we're not alert to the enemy, we can begin to think "too highly of ourselves."

How do we counter this as we walk as Christ's disciples? In humility we obey the command to take the time to honestly think about who we are, and know that God has given each of us the faith to do that. This leads to our fourth discipleship principle.

4) Humble Service – "It was just before the Passover Festival. Jesus knew that the hour had come for him to leave this world and go to the Father. Having loved his own who were in the world, he loved them to the end... Jesus knew that the Father had put all things under his power, and that he had come from God and was returning to God; so he got up from the meal, took off his outer clothing, and wrapped a towel around his waist. After that, he poured water into a basin and began to wash his disciples' feet, drying them with the towel that was wrapped around him... When he had finished washing their feet, he put on his clothes and returned to his place. 'Do you understand what I have done for you?' he asked them. 'You call me Teacher and Lord, and rightly so, for that is what I am. Now that I, your Lord and Teacher, have washed your feet, you also should wash one another's feet. I have set you an example that you should do as I have done for you. Very truly I tell you, no servant is greater than his master, nor is a messenger greater than the one who sent him. Now that you know these things, you will be blessed if you do them.'" (John 13:1, 3-5; 12-17; also see Philippians 2:3-8)

Every relationship begins with our disciple relationship with Christ as Lord. His teaching and modeling lays the foundation and sets the stage for our discipleship walk in Him. Here are four key elements from the John 13 text above calling us as His disciples to humble service:

A) Love – Jesus showed them His full and complete love (v. 1). As His disciples we should pay close attention to what happens next.

B) Humility – He knew He was from God, returning to God, and God had placed all things in His hands (authority) (v. 3). Remember this is the essence of humility, which is knowing with confidence and contentment who you are in Christ so you can place others above yourself. I asked the Lord several years ago as I was studying and praying through this, "Why would you tell us this about Christ?" Very plainly The Spirit placed these thoughts in my mind: "I want you to know that Christ knew Who He was because of what He was getting ready to do." Christ modeled humility. What was He getting ready to do?

C) Service/Servant's Heart – Jesus got up from the table and began to wash all the disciples' feet (vv. 4-5). This is what loving humility looks like and we will struggle to practice it in our selfish pride if we do not know who we are in Christ. He doesn't stop there.

D) Authority – After washing their feet Jesus does something that should stop us in our tracks when it comes to understanding love, humility, service, and discipleship. He literally calls attention to what He has done and instead of saying, "There, that's love and humble service," He recalls for the 11 remaining disciples that they know Him as Master. What does this imply? That Jesus is the Authority in their eyes and He confirms it: "You are right, that's what I am." (vv. 12-13)

In one loving act of humble service and with a question and statement, Jesus tells His disciples, then and now, that love, humility, a servant's heart, and authority cannot be separated in My Kingdom. WOW! This is powerful and speaks to how we should live as His disciples everywhere we are called and placed in this culture and world for His Kingdom and Glory.

He finishes by describing discipleship. "Do as I have done for you and you will be blessed" (vv. 14-17...my paraphrase). Live as a humble servant of your Master.

Again these are all repeated in principle in the beautiful condensed Gospel story and our call to imitate Christ found in Philippians 2: Sacrificial love and a humble servant's heart (vv. 6-8); Blessing and authority (vv. 9-11); our discipleship call to be like Him (vv. 3-5).

These are certainly not easy in our flesh. Actually they're impossible in our flesh! That's why we must follow through and sacrifice our renewed and holy lives in Christ back to God. As His disciples, it's how we live and move and have our being.

Brother Rick Warren wrote Purpose-Driven Life, in which he outlines how we can know how God has called us by our **SHAPE**.

Spiritual gifts
Heart/passion
Aptitude/ability
Passion/heart
Experience/education

It was an excellent book as many millions can attest. I would simply add one thing that I feel confident Brother Warren would agree with: While our SHAPE reveals how God made us and what He has made us for, according to His Word, the only way we'll fully know His will is to sacrifice our SHAPE back to Him (see Romans 12:1-2 again). There is a huge difference in maturity between telling The Lord what we are going to do for Him, and sacrificing back to Him what He has given us with a heart that says, "Here am I, do as you please in and through me."

CHAPTER 10

PRACTICAL APPLICATION: LIVING AS CHRIST'S DISCIPLES

How Will We Know?

God's Word makes it very clear what we are called to be as Christ's disciples. It is also obvious in His Word that this can only be done by His changing our hearts as we accept Him as Savior AND LORD.

So what does it look like? If our hearts are truly changed and The Holy Spirit is dwelling in us, then how will we know? How do we apply the Scriptural principles of discipleship in practice? For that matter, what are the Biblical principles that make His Lordship and our discipleship evident in our lives and to others?

While volumes could be filled detailing scriptural principles, I will focus on nine key applications to be practiced by all disciples. Before I do, however, I must explain something I learned as an athlete that is crucial in any discipline—spiritual, physical, mental or relational.

One year in college after our season was over I decided to take a break from my regular workouts. Well, two weeks turned into a month. A month turned into two and then to four, and suddenly we were six weeks out from preseason.

No problem. I'd just head to the gym and weight room each day and be ready to go. My mistake? Not that I was very prideful, but I just knew, and was going to prove, that I could still lift the same amount and run as fast as I had four months ago. I can see you grimacing now.

I did just that. I pushed myself to lift and run what I had at the end of the previous season and felt great, for the next few hours. When I woke up the next day (and the following day), I literally could not walk, run, sit, stand or even eat. I kid you not, for two days every time I tried to lift an eating utensil to my mouth my entire arm, side and back cramped up. It was an extremely painful but lifelong lesson.

What did I learn?

Maturity requires discipline and discipline requires manageability and commitment. No matter what we attempt, whether physical as evidenced by my story, mental as evidenced by every test you've taken, or spiritual in growing in Christ, in order to learn and grow, we must remain committed to those priorities and principles in His Word. And in order to do that we must make it manageable.

If we had the strength to do it all at once the first time, why would we ever need to go into the weight room? If we already knew His Word and will, why would we ever need to step into His spiritual weight room (or disciplines)?

> ### *We must make our commitment manageable*
> ### *to mature as His disciples.*

How does this apply to spiritual disciplines? I try to answer that here with Scriptures for your study and application. The first six deal with personal discipleship and the last three with discipleship in relationships and fellowship as Christ's Church.

Before I share these, let me explain that these words were written as clear commands to be obeyed. The Scriptures calling us to apply the disciplines of discipleship were not given as suggestions, they were, and are, commands to be followed in loving obedience (John 14:15). I include brief explanations with these Scriptures and trust The Holy Spirit to compel, encourage, and strengthen you to loving obedience.

God has many commands that all deal with His love for us and us loving Him...He has no demands! They require willful surrender in loving obedience to know all He has in store for us!

Personal Discipleship Applications (Emphasis added)

1) Bible Study – "Study and do your best to present yourself to God approved, a workman [tested by trial] who has no reason to be ashamed, accurately handling and skillfully teaching the word of truth." (2 Timothy 2:15 AMP); "Hear, O Israel! The LORD is our God, the LORD is one! You shall love the LORD your God with all your heart and with all your soul and with all your might. These words, which I am commanding you today, shall be on your heart. You shall teach them diligently to your sons and shall talk of them when you sit in your house and when you walk by the way and when you lie down and when you rise up." (Deuteronomy 6:4-7 NASB)

Spend time in God's Word. If you choose to use a devotional, be sure to choose one where Scripture as God's Word is of absolute importance and ask The Spirit to teach, lead and fill you. "Let the word of Christ richly dwell within you, with all wisdom teaching and admonishing one another with psalms and hymns and spiritual songs, singing with thankfulness in your hearts to God." (Colossians 3:16 NASB); "And do not get drunk with wine, for that is dissipation, but be filled with the Spirit." (Ephesians 5:18 NASB)

2) Prayer – "Do not be anxious about anything, but in every situation, by prayer and petition, with thanksgiving, present your requests to God." (Philippians 4:6); "Pray continually." (1 Thessalonians 5:17); "And pray in the Spirit on all occasions with all kinds of prayers and requests. With this in mind, be alert and always keep on praying for all the Lord's people." (Ephesians 6:18)

A simple process to remember when praying is C.A.T.S.: Confession; Adoration/praise; Thanksgiving; Supplication for self and intercession for others. One final thought regarding prayer and relationships in general: "Husbands, in the same way be considerate as you live with your wives, and treat them with respect as the weaker partner and as heirs with you of the gracious gift of life, so that nothing will hinder your prayers." (1 Peter 3:7) The relationship with your spouse is crucial to God hearing and responding.

3) Quiet Time, Reflection, Meditation – "He says, 'Be still, and know that I am God; I will be exalted among the nations, I will be exalted in the earth.'" (Psalm 46:10) "May these words of my mouth and this meditation of my heart be pleasing in your sight, LORD, my Rock and my Redeemer." (Psalm 1 9:14) Psalm 119—22 sections of eight verses based on the Hebrew alphabet—offers an excellent set of Scriptures to help you meditate and reflect. It will help you appreciate and desire God's Word.

4) Communion – This includes not only the sacred time spent in what many churches call Communion or Eucharist, but also growing in the discipline of communion with other believers. The first is Paul's recounting of Christ's establishing the Holy Communion: "For I received from the Lord what I also passed on to you: The Lord Jesus, on the night he was betrayed, took bread, and when he had given thanks, he broke it and said, 'This is my body, which is for you; do this in remembrance of me.' In the same way, after supper he took the cup, saying, 'This cup is the new covenant in my blood; do this, whenever you drink it, in remembrance of me.' For whenever you eat this bread and drink this cup, you proclaim the Lord's death until

he comes. So then, whoever eats the bread or drinks the cup of the Lord in an unworthy manner will be guilty of sinning against the body and blood of the Lord. Everyone ought to examine themselves before they eat of the bread and drink from the cup. For those who eat and drink without discerning the body of Christ eat and drink judgment on themselves. That is why many among you are weak and sick, and a number of you have fallen asleep. But if we were more discerning with regard to ourselves, we would not come under such judgment." (1 Corinthians 11:23-31). This second reference is the command to the believers' fellowship with others: "They devoted themselves to the apostles' teaching and to fellowship, to the breaking of bread and to prayer." (Acts 2:42)

5) Sabbath – Under Old Testament law, breaking the Sabbath was an offense punishable by death. The early Church shifted the focus of worship and all it involved to the first day of the week to commemorate Christ's Resurrection on that day and likely also to allow them as Jews to continue observing the lawful Sabbath.

The key is to be obedient to the command of the Sabbath that served to recognize two things: that God is Holy and we are not; that in our unholiness and weakness there is a need for rest, to put aside pride in our strength, and observe the Sabbath. "By the seventh day God had finished the work he had been doing; so on the seventh day he rested from all his work. Then God blessed the seventh day and made it holy, because on it he rested from all the work of creating that he had done." (Genesis 2:2-3); "Remember the Sabbath day by keeping it holy." (Exodus 20:8)

6) Fasting – While not commanded, fasting is a powerful spiritual discipline. Generally, we fast from food, but it can also mean not partaking of anything from which we draw strength, satisfaction or pleasure, so we can more fully depend on The Holy Spirit and God's Word. "While they were worshiping the Lord and fasting, the Holy Spirit said, 'Set apart for me Barnabas and Saul for the work to which I have called them.'" (Acts 13:2); "Paul and Barnabas appointed elders for them in each church and, with prayer and fasting, committed them to the Lord, in whom they had put their trust." (14:23); When Jesus cast out a demon His disciples had not able to they asked Him why? "He replied, 'This kind can come out only by prayer and fasting.'" (Mark 9:29)

As we grow and mature as Christ's disciples individually, His Word is very clear that we are also to be growing and maturing in our relationships with other believers.

Here are three more spiritual disciplines that help us do that:

7) Worship – God alone is worthy of our personal and collective worship and praise: "You shall have no other gods before me. You shall not make for yourself an image in the form of anything in heaven above or on the earth beneath or in the waters below. You shall not bow down to them or worship them; for I, the LORD your God, am a jealous God, punishing the children for the sin of the parents to the third and fourth generation of those who hate me, but showing love to a thousand generations of those who love me and keep my commandments. You shall not misuse the name of the LORD your God, for the LORD will not hold anyone guiltless who misuses his name." (Exodus 20:3-7); "Hear, O Israel! The LORD is our God, the LORD is one! Love the LORD your God with all your heart and with all your soul and with all your strength." (Deuteronomy 6:4-5); "Jesus answered, 'It is written: Worship the Lord your God and serve him only.'" (Luke 4:8); "God is spirit, and his worshipers must worship in the Spirit and in truth." (John 4:24)

8) Giving/Serving – "Remember this: Whoever sows sparingly will also reap sparingly, and whoever sows generously will also reap generously. Each of you should give what you have decided in your heart to give, not reluctantly or under compulsion, for God loves a cheerful giver. And God is able to bless you abundantly, so that in all things at all times, having all that you need, you will abound in every good work." (2 Corinthians 9:6-8)

As by the power of the Holy Spirit we grow and mature personally and relationally as Christ's disciples, we become more like Christ and the world sees His Truth and love in our individual lives and in The Church. If they are not seeing it in us, individually and collectively, then we need to ask whether we are walking as His disciples.

9) Fellowship/Relationship/Church – "They devoted themselves to the apostles' teaching and to fellowship, to the breaking of bread and to prayer." (Acts 2:42) "And let us consider how we may spur one another on toward love and good deeds, not

giving up meeting together, as some are in the habit of doing, but encouraging one another— and all the more as you see the Day approaching." (Hebrews 10:24-25) Discipleship builds our faithful testimony, which spills over into reaching a lost and hurting world with His message in fulfilling the Great Commission. "Then Jesus came to them and said, 'All authority in heaven and on earth has been given to me. Therefore go and make disciples of all nations, baptizing them in the name of the Father and of the Son and of the Holy Spirit, and teaching them to obey everything I have commanded you. And surely I am with you always, to the very end of the age.'" (Matthew 28:18-20)

Without discipline there are no disciples and no discipleship!
Without The Holy Spirit we have no spiritual discipline!

I feel so strongly about this that I'm going to repeat what I stated earlier. These are not suggestions or recommendations. These are commands that need to be kept for all those who desire to walk as Christ's disciples and with Him as Lord.

Don't try to do what I did in the weight room and arrive "fully mature" all at once—we just can't do that. That's why it's called discipleship and requires patience and time.

Early on, I began each day in God's Word for 15 minutes. You may be able to do the same, less or more. For most who have never practiced these disciplines or tried to do them all at once and burned out, here's a simple formula: Adjust the time to work for you. Do this and God will honor it. Your time with and growth in Him and His Word will be greatly rewarded.

BEGIN WITH 5 MINUTES EVERY DAY AND DON'T MISS ONE DAY!

The Next Step: Discipleship

Now that you've gotten the key to walking in the spiritual disciplines of His Word, the next step is to begin praying about and discipling or helping others do the same—not only the practical steps but also a deeper dive into His Word to grow as His disciples.

As I began to spend time with Him, in His Word and prayer and applying these disciplines, I was compelled more and more to encourage others. Early on in this process, for some reason the number 10 kept coming to my mind. I dismissed it for a while but it persisted and I began to pray about it.

As I prayed I sensed the Lord was giving me that number to remind me that I needed to be discipling others but not to spread myself too thin or pridefully take on too many.

So as I began discipling I kept this in mind and began to form the boundaries that helped me best pour into others. I would not disciple in any one season more than 10 men.

When Ami and I married I continued but I reduced the number to eight and I counted a couple as one (as that is how they are defined in God's Word). God rewarded this by keeping between four and eight men or couples without it ever being too burdensome on me and especially on our marriage.

I did the same by reducing the number by one as each of our children were born and kept it there until they left for college. The principle here is that my wife and children, according to God's Word, take priority as those I'm discipling. As my children left for college I added spots back until I reached 10.

God honored this as I have honored Him in keeping my priorities in line with His Word. Ten was my number and it may be more or less for you, but remember the priorities and principles of keeping your marriage, spouse, and family first.

"Paul's idea of service is the same as Our Lord's:
'I am among you as He that serveth'; 'ourselves your servants
for Jesus' sake...' The mainspring of Paul's service is not love for
men, but love for Jesus Christ. If we are devoted to the cause
of humanity, we shall soon be crushed and broken-hearted,
for we shall often meet with more ingratitude from men than we
would from a dog; but if our motive is love to God, no ingratitude
can hinder us from serving our fellow men...no matter how men
may treat me, they will never treat me with the spite and hatred
with which I treated Jesus Christ. When we realize that Jesus
Christ has served us to the end of our meanness, our selfishness,
and sin, nothing that we meet with from others can exhaust
our determination to serve men for His sake."

— Oswald Chambers, *My Utmost for His Highest*

CHAPTER 11

A JUDGMENT DAY PARABLE: LORDSHIP, DISCIPLESHIP & RELATIONSHIP

As I wrap up these foundational chapters on Authority, Christ's Lordship, and our discipleship, allow me to share a modern day parable that The Lord gave me in a clear vision that depicts His words in Matthew 7:21-23, "Not everyone who says to me, 'Lord, Lord,' will enter the kingdom of heaven, but only the one who does the will of my Father who is in heaven. Many will say to me on that day, 'Lord, Lord, did we not prophesy in your name and in your name drive out demons and in your name perform many miracles?' Then I will tell them plainly, 'I never knew you. Away from me, you evildoers!'" These should be perhaps the most chilling, challenging and motivating words, reminding us of what it means to be in relationship with Him, walk as His disciple, and build every other relationship on that foundation.

Here we have Christ's powerful prophecy on the absolute importance of Relationship and Eternity—first, He died to freely place all believers in a relationship with Him which can only be Lord and disciple; second, this is lived out in our relationship with others. So often we get the cart before the horse by thinking that just by being given this relationship with God we have already matured and completed the first and greatest command: "Love the Lord your God with all your heart, mind, soul and strength." (Matthew 22:37-38)

His command points to the reality that we absolutely must prioritize this loving relationship with Him. Then we can begin to show this love in our service toward others and in so doing show God's love for them and us.

One of the most repeated messages to encourage members and attendees in service to their fellow humankind is for pastors to ask them to find ways to go above and beyond in their service and giving. This is a wonderful idea that we need to be willing to do, but we must remember Christ's strong warning in Matthew 7:21-23.

One night after one of these sermons, I was reflecting on what had been shared and I truly believe The Holy Spirit gave me the following vision.

A Judgment Day Parable

I was standing in line at Christ's Judgment throne. When it was my turn, He graciously spoke, "Hi, Greg." I was a little taken aback although I shouldn't have been. That may have been my first clue, but I proceeded to pull out a long list of things I'd done to show my love for others.

Two in particular stood out so I exclaimed, "Jesus, check this out. Our pastor told us that to show others Your Love, the next time I was in the drive-thru line to just randomly pay for the person's meal behind me and leave a little for the cashier. I decided to really show them Your love and paid for three carloads behind me. Shortly after that my wife and I were on a date night and, being on a tight budget, we went to Outback with a 25% off coupon.

"Our waitress Nina was a frail, fairly young lady who looked worn-out but smiled and gave us wonderful service. We left her a $100 bill on a $40 ticket! I wrote on a napkin and laid it on top of the tip so she'd be surprised when she found it. I had noticed that when we gave her the discount coupon her smile faded and I bet she was thinking, 'Oh no, another reduced ticket...and tip.'

"Boy was she in for a surprise due to our showing her Your love. We slipped away from the table but I lingered to see her reaction and of course get the satisfaction of having served so wonderfully. She almost missed it.

"The wonderful smile turned into a near-snarl as she looked at the napkin, quickly read it, and crumpled it up. Then she saw the $100, but instead of smiling, she began to cry. She uncrumpled the napkin and just looked at it. I didn't fully understand it, but I knew we'd shown her Your love."

"Really?" Jesus asked.

"Of course," I replied, "and there's much more where that came from." I had to show Jesus how much I'd done in serving Him and others and, of course, that I belonged in Heaven.

He interrupted and said, "Greg, that's enough. I don't need to see or hear any more: you're a sinner and you must depart from me for all of Eternity because you never knew me. We never had a relationship. You did all this stuff that you were told to do, but you never spent the time to get to know Me."

He said this with a combination of matter-of-fact truth like I should have known it was coming and great sadness with the reality that I didn't.

"But I'm saved," I said. "I've been baptized, prayed the prayer, served my fellow man to show them I loved them and that You did as well. My ministers and pastors told me that's what it looks like to be a Christian. So surely I'm good and get to be in Heaven."

I was fading into the distance and He heard no more from me.

As I staggered away into eternal darkness and torment I heard a familiar voice and looked to see who was next in line.

Jesus welcomed her, "Hello, Nina." Nina—I knew I recognized that voice and frail form—began to weep. Between sobs she said, "Jesus, I don't have a list like that tall guy did. All I can do is tell you my story.

"I was a waitress at Outback. One evening a tall, goofy guy came in with his beautiful wife and they were seated at my table. As they paid I noticed they had a 25% off coupon and I knew that almost always meant very little in tips for me. They left and when I came back, sure enough, they had left just a napkin that said 'Jesus loves you' on it.

"Well they had no way of knowing but I learned that you did. I was behind on several bills and had received a third warning that the electric was going to be cut off if I didn't pay my $95 utility bill the next day. You knew that I was a single mom with two illegitimate children by two fathers. As I crumpled up the napkin, cussing them and you under my breath, I saw a $100 bill.

"I just stopped in my tracks because I knew it was a miracle. It was the dead of a very cold winter and I had no idea what I was going to do for my children and me, but You provided. I uncrumpled the napkin and looked at those words again.

"From that day on, Jesus, I came to know you and spent the rest of my life getting to know and love you more. I passed it on to my children who both married and I continued to share you with my grandchildren. I don't have a list..."

Jesus politely interrupted, "Nina, I know all of this and you don't need a list. I know that you know Me. I know that you passed it on to your children and grandchildren just as The Father and I designed it to happen. Well done, Nina. You are a good and faithful servant. Enter into all The Father has prepared for you."

Nina joyously ran into the Heavenly Kingdom with a huge smile as I, drifting further into the darkness and torment, yelled out, "But that's Nina. She's the Outback waitress that I helped save. If she gets in then surely so should I!"

But it was too late. I never knew Him and she did. And that's what makes all the difference both in this life and for Eternity.

There are millions of people, made in God's image, who serve their fellow man every year around the globe as an overflow of their fleshly compassion, but they do not know Jesus as their Lord. Many sit in our churches. Our service must be more than just a fleshly, compassionate response. It must be an overflow of our surrender, sacrifice, and obedience to Christ as Lord as we share His Truth by our lives as His disciples. Otherwise, we risk adding to the multitude that do not know Jesus, as He prophesied in Matthew 7:21-23.

Is He your Savior and Lord? His Word is very clear that He has saved you to be in relationship with Him and the only way you can be in that relationship is to know Him as Lord, as His disciple. Don't miss out by claiming Him as Savior and not knowing Him as Lord.

Every other relationship will reflect whether He is Lord of your life or not. You can be assured that He is and that He is blessing you to be a blessing to others as you serve Him and them. That's how discipleship is lived out—in relationships.

STUDY GUIDE
DISCIPLESHIP...OUR RESPONSE
TO HIS LORDSHIP

Key Concepts

1) Salvation is free and places us in a relationship with God that we could have no other way.

2) Discipleship requires commitment and a cost on our part with Christ as Lord.

3) Christ as Lord means that He must take first priority in every part of our life.

4) Being a disciple of Christ requires that I die to my own selfish interests.

5) Honorable submission, honest surrender, holy sacrifice and humble service characterize the life of a disciple of Christ.

6) As Christ's disciple I'm called to sacrifice the life that He saved back to Him.

7) Discipleship requires that I practice personal and relational disciplines found in God's Word by the power of His Holy Spirit.

8) A disciple of Christ develops and practices habits and disciplines to live wisely and build good relationships in Christ and by The Holy Spirit.

9) Discipleship is first and foremost about knowing, loving and serving God so that we can then love and serve our fellow man.

Questions

1) How have you been taught to view salvation and discipleship?

2) Is Christ first (Lord) in every part of your life?

3) Christ as Lord means that He must take first priority in every part of our life.

4) How do you see the four Biblical principles from Christ's life in yours?

      a. Honorable submission

      b. Honest surrender

      c. Holy sacrifice

      d. Humble service

5) Are you consistently practicing spiritual applications in your personal life? (Bible study, prayer, quiet time, Sabbath, communion and fasting)

6) Are you consistently practicing spiritual applications in your relational life? (Worship, giving/serving and fellowship/relationship)

7) What disciplines/boundaries (spiritual, personal, relational, etc.) do you need to develop as a disciple of Christ in your life and relationships?

Discussion

1) What virtues of Christ mentioned above do you see in your life?

2) What virtues of Christ can you build in your life?

3) What's the greatest hindrance in your life to your being a disciple of Christ?

4) What will you change in order to make Him Lord and be His disciple?

Action Items

1) Begin today to set aside five minutes each day to read God's Word, pray and ask Him to teach you. Don't get discouraged. You can give God five minutes and watch Him work in and through your life as you are faithful. Make it manageable so you can keep the commitment every day.

2) Find a Bible-believing and teaching church and get connected to other Christ followers.

SECTION 4

RELATIONSHIPS...
WHAT WE WERE
CREATED FOR

*"The answer lies in a personal relationship
to Jesus Christ...We can ever remain powerless,
as were the disciples, by trying to do God's work
not in concentration on His power, but by ideas drawn
from our own temperament. We slander God by our
very eagerness to work for Him without knowing Him...
This is your line of service — to see that there is
nothing between Jesus and yourself. Is there?"*

— Oswald Chambers, *My Utmost for His Highest*

Disguising Godly Relationships

Several years ago, I was asked to speak for the final three weeks of a four-week series at a large men's gathering. The topic was "Men, Lust/ Porn and Relationships." Craig Gross of XXX Church kicked off the first week. Usual attendance at this weekly gathering ran about 250-300. During this series there were 450-500 men each week.

After teaching my first week on pursuing a loving relationship with God, I followed up the next week with how to build a Godly, fulfilling marriage and family. I was challenging the men to be sure they were prioritizing their lives, marriage, spouse and family according to God's covenant order.

In the middle of sharing, The Spirit laid a question on my heart about an upcoming Promise Keepers (PK) conference: "How many of you are planning to attend the PK Conference in a couple of weekends?"

Let me just say, I'm a big PK fan, as were many in the group. Nearly two-thirds of the 450+ in attendance excitedly raised their hands showing their commitment to be Godly men. The Spirit immediately prompted me to ask a follow up question. My initial thought was, "REALLY? You want me to ask that?" Yet I knew why He was prompting me to do so. "OK," I silently agreed and took a deep breath...

CHAPTER 12

THE CURRENCY OF CHRIST'S KINGDOM: LOVING RELATIONSHIPS

If the Shoe Fits, Wear It

One of the more poignant questions we need to ask is "How are we doing when it comes to building loving relationships as His disciples—first in our homes and families, and then in His Church?"

As you finish this section and the story begun above, let me simply say: If the shoe fits, wear it. If it doesn't, then help those it does fit.

The currency of the culture is obviously money, but money is only a means to an end. It allows us to obtain, afford, or satisfy ourselves with fame, stuff, security and/or pleasure—or avoid those things that don't offer these. The outcomes serve as the real "currency" of the world and they are always at the expense of our relationship with others.

The currency of Christ's Kingdom is loving relationships and they are nearly always built at the expense of the stuff of this world! What are you investing in? People...or pleasure, success and stuff?

Our discipleship response to Christ must be lived out in relationship, and not just in relationship to Him as Lord. It is to be lived out in such a way that being His disciple impacts and influences every other person and relationship in our lives.

However, as we have seen throughout this book, God's Word is also very clear (Deuteronomy 6:4-6; Jeremiah 29:12-13; Matthew 22:37-39; Mark 12:29-31) that His covenant order has a distinct priority in how we are to live in relationship with Him and with others so we can have the greatest impact with His currency—loving relationships.

Unfortunately, the enemy knows all too well the contrast of these two currencies. Throughout time and history—but never as prevalent as today—his greatest weapon against loving relationships is "porneia."

I've heard but never been able to verify that Hugh Hefner said, "The reason I've been so successful in this business (porn) is because the Church has done such a horrible job with sexuality!" Whether he said it or not, the statement is accurate and this must change.

It's not enough for the church to simply speak for marriage, purity and moral relationships based on God's Word. We must hold Christ's followers accountable to this as a priority if we are to see loving relationships across the board. We also must boldly speak and stand against relational and sexual immorality and do so with grace, gentleness, and respect. Only then will we see loving relationships, healthy marriages and families, and strong churches.

Loving Relationships vs. Stuff/Success

God's Word calls us to seek His Kingdom and Righteousness first (Matthew 6:33) and to focus on that which is eternal rather than temporal (2 Corinthians 4:18). These commands prompt us to explore what The Holy Spirit means in His Word when He speaks of eternal or Kingdom things to ensure that we understand where we are to invest our lives.

I can find only three things on this temporal earth that are Kingdom in nature. They are:

1)   God's Holy Spirit;
2)   God's Word and;
3)   the souls of human beings.

Everything else is temporary and will pass away. Only these three will remain and they all exist for relationship.

My question to you: "What are you doing with His Word, His Spirit, and the lives of those around you? Are you investing in what will last or in that which will someday perish?"

God's Word shows a very clear contrast between His design and desire for loving relationships and the world's attraction to stuff and self at the expense of true relationships. The two words in Scripture that best describe love are hesed in Hebrew (Old Testament) and agape in Greek (New Testament).

Both words describe God's unconditional, sacrificial, selfless love. All expressions of love find their source in Him (1 John 4:19). We call many things love that aren't!

On the other hand, porneia is the Greek word from which we derive "pornography" and stands for any and all sexual immorality. In Scriptural context it includes a sexually immoral mindset evident in sexual sin.

There are many fleshly lusts and desires that destroy hearts, minds and relationships— jealousy, envy, anger, pride to name just a few (see Galatians 5:16-19). They all play a role and many are encompassed in porneia, which is the enemy's greatest ammunition in this battle. For this reason I focus on porneia with the understanding that all other vices and "lusts of the flesh" must be accounted for in our lives and, along with porneia, must be overcome by Christ and in His Word and Spirit as we choose to nurture relationships and build His Kingdom.

Keep all of this in mind as you compare and contrast God's covenant order in relationships and sexuality as shown in Scripture with the way of the world. The Scriptures below show the standard that God has established for human relationships and sexuality in His Kingdom as well as the perversion of the enemy that prevails in our human nature apart from Christ. We have a choice to make, personally and relationally, when it comes to whether we will follow the loving disciplines of His Word and Spirit or the lustful desires of our flesh.

Following is a straightforward description from God's Word contrasting His Kingdom with the world and our flesh regarding relationships, sexuality and community...

RELATIONSHIPS

Kingdom Currency – Loving Relationships

Christ as Lord – Hesed/Agape

- Fruits of the Spirit (Galatians 5:22-23)
- Personally (Proverbs 31:10-31; I Corinthians 13:4-8a)
- In Home (Ephesians 5:21-33)
- In Church (Book of I John)
- In Community (Matthew 22:37-39; 5:43-44)
- Parable of Sower (Matthew 13:3-9; 18-23) (emphasis v. 23)

World's Currency – Stuff/Success

Satan ("Self") as lord – Lust and selfish desire

- Lusts of the flesh (Galatians 5:16-21)
- Parable of Sower (Matthew 13:3-9; 18-23) (emphasis vv. 19-22)
- Selfishness, flesh and world (Romans 1:18-31; Galatians 6:7-8a)

SEXUALITY

Kingdom Currency - Christ as Lord – Agape

- Marriage as One Woman, One Man (Genesis 2:24; Matthew 19:5-6)
- Our bodies as part of Body of Christ, Temple of Holy Spirit (I Corinthians 5:13; 6:19)
- Sexual Purity and Blessing (I Corinthians 6:18; Ephesians 5:3)

World's Currency – Satan ("Self") as lord – Porneia

- Depravity of man (all sexual sin) (Romans 1 – emphasis vv. 18-32)
- Lusts of the flesh (Galatians 5:16-19)
- Lust, Sin, Death (James 1:15)

"Flee from sexual immorality. All other sins a person commits are outside the body, but whoever sins sexually, sins against their own body." (1 Corinthians 6:18)

Understand that there is a difference between a stronghold and a struggle. A stronghold is something that you have given into. It is set up in your heart and mind, controlling or dictating your thoughts and actions. You may say you desire God's love in your life but continually choose the lust of the flesh or the eyes, or the pride of life (1 John 2:15-17) over and over again. This is a stronghold, and porneia is perhaps the strongest.

You can never win and hesed/agape cannot reign in your life if you continue to willingly give in to porneia or any stronghold. You must recognize it, quit deceiving yourself, and surrender it to The Holy Spirit to conquer. Otherwise it will cripple and destroy your life and every relationship.

A struggle is something you battle against because you are aware of it and do not desire to have it in your life. For this reason, you may struggle with porneia or any of the lusts of the flesh, lusts of the eyes, or pride of life, but you fight against it. Know that as a Christ follower you already have the victory! Even though you may struggle, you will overcome if you continue to walk in faith—believe in God's overcoming Truth and act accordingly, even when you struggle.

Hesed/Agape and Porneia/Lust cannot willingly exist together in your heart. One or the other will win out. Which are you choosing?

CHAPTER 13

LOVE & LUST...
PORNOGRAPHY & PORNEIA

One Couple's Battle with Porn/Porneia

They had been in my office several times and, while there was improvement, it was evident that there was still a lot of tension. They met online after previous marriages—one had lost a spouse to cancer, the other to drugs and affairs.

The husband attended a long-term residential sexual addiction/ pornography treatment facility prior to their marriage, admittedly so they could get married and begin having sex. Not surprisingly, problems had continued and most of them were centered on porneia.

Now they were on the brink of a divorce that neither wanted, as they desired to honor The Lord. We established accountability practices and placed blocks on every computer and phone, including exchanging a smart phone for a flip-up with no access to Internet. After several meetings, things were improving.

Before they arrived for a scheduled meeting, I received a text that she knew he was still looking at porn. She'd "caught" him that day.

He had called me and said he didn't want to go home because he knew it would just be more of the same—accusations, angry words, fighting, and then isolation.

As they recounted the day's events, she was convinced he was still actively pursuing porn and had just found ways to hide it. I asked her, "Is there any proof over the last three months of porn use?" She could produce no evidence.

It was obvious from his slumped posture and downcast look that he was a beaten man. He'd told her he was not involved in porn and had not looked at it for more than three months.

I could tell that her woman's/wife's intuition was strong and that there was an issue. I could also tell that he was telling her the truth. I shared what The Spirit had laid on my heart.

I began by looking at her and stating that I fully believed him. My individual meetings with him had revealed that he truly desired to rid himself of this porn "demon." I also reassured her that there was still something he was struggling with and that is why she was noticing the frustration and distance. He was not engaging in porn, as the world and enemy would have us see it in active pursuit and participation with videos, magazines, or screens. He had been faithful in that regard.

He was encouraged by my comments to her. However, I looked at him and asked, "While you're not pursuing porn as defined just now, you are still struggling with the videos and photos that play over and over in your mind. Is that a fair statement?"

He looked down and nodded. It was not easy, but she was reassured that he was not seeking out porn and was willing to walk through that struggle for the porneia in his mind. They would do this by renewing the mind (Romans 12:2), and taking thoughts captive and making them obedient to Christ (2 Corinthians 10:4-5), along with continued accountability and help.

His face softened for the first time in a long time and he shared with her that with The Lord's help and hers, he would get through this and be the husband that she wanted him to be.

They moved out of state a few years ago, but my last report from them was that they were doing very well and enjoying retirement together in the peace, Love, and Lordship of Jesus Christ.

The Cookie Jar – A Satire on Love

Picture yourself as a parent with your children, gathered around the dinner table nearly finished with the meal. The children are struggling to clean their plates, so you grab a jar out of the pantry and take the top off. The aroma is intoxicating and the children want what's in that jar!

You say, "If you clean up all the green things on your plate you can have one of these." So with a few veggies under the table, some in the dog's belly, and a few making their way slowly down the child's throat, the plate is finally clean!

"Gimme, gimme, gimme," say the children and you lovingly oblige. It's not until later when the dog throws up that the parents realize that not all the green things ended up where they were supposed to. But, some were eaten and the children got a treat and enjoyed it. What parent doesn't want to be a part of that?

So what happens next? Well you sit the kids down and ask them if they would like to learn how to get into the cookie jar whenever they wanted. After all, the most loving thing would be to give them all the cookies they want, right?

"Watch carefully," you say.

You place the jar in the corner cabinet behind the flour and then explain, "You need to be very careful as you climb on the counter. You know you're not supposed to be there so if you hear us coming down the stairs jump down and act like nothing happened."

"Once on the counter, you very slowly slide the flour bag to the side. If you push the bag too quickly the flour will blow out and get on the door, the cabinet, and the counter and we'll know you've been in the cookie jar.

"Now that you have it, eat as many as you want! Whoever gets the most...good for them!"

Of course it doesn't work this way. How many of you had to be taught to stay out of the cookie jar, maybe with a slight slap on the hand?

It's completely silly, thus the satire. Love is not giving our children all the cookies they want; that's unhealthy and unloving. We give them cookies sparingly to enjoy without health risks and we teach them to share and give to others.

Because children don't fully know or understand that "too much of a good thing" can be very bad for you, we teach them the discipline of keeping their hands out of the jar as well as the concept of sharing once they've been given these wonderful treats. Both the discipline and the sharing are concepts rooted in love that we must learn or we will not know how to love.

I've seen numerous couples dating, living together, or married that have never been taught what it means to truly love.

The Cookie Jar Explained

Stick with me as I explain. How many of you were born selfless? I hope no one raised his or her hand. How many of you were born selfish? I hope all of you raised your hands. We are all born selfish and that must be overcome to love and build good relationships. The natural inclination, as with the cookie jar, is that once we've found something we like we want all we can get with little or no desire to share.

While you can do cookies that way as a selfish person, at least until you run out, you can't do relationships that way. We have to be taught to be selfless, and if we are not or we hold onto our selfish nature, it will show up in every relationship. What does that look like? If you're still not putting together the satire of The Cookie Jar, here it is.

I've seen numerous couples in relationship and even walking down the wedding aisle with their imaginary cookie jars tucked under their outside arms. They've learned this is "love:"

"I'll give you one cookie if you give me two."

Literally, I've seen this over and over. People are seldom, if ever, taught that the only way Love really works—sticking with our cookie jar analogy—is when we learn to say, "Here, you can have all my cookies. That's what I think of you, whether you give me any cookies or not." Obviously if you find someone not willing to share or give of themselves it's not likely they are ready for a loving relationship.

Eventually you'll figure out that those who never learned to love don't share or give away their cookies without demanding more in return than were given. You realize that this won't work. Over time the one who demands more than they give will realize the person they've demanded from has run out—so they move on to the next person.

Here's the bottom line seen from the perspective of God's hesed/agape love:

Love is not give and take. Love is give, period! Only when I learn to die to my selfishness and be willing to unconditionally give myself for the sake of others will I ever be able to love. This is a lifelong pursuit.

That's what Jesus did. He said, "Here, you can have all that I am. I give my all to and for you." He doesn't demand or coerce, He just loves. The only way we can know that is to know Him and learn to love as He does.

With regard to dating, porneia/lust and love, remember that you must first learn and begin to die to self in order to love. Then, not only can you love, but you can also help others know what it is and recognize it in others. No matter what you see in another, no matter how "hot" they are or how much they may turn you on, remember that love is not a feeling. Love is a commitment, a choice, and an act of will. And that is why discipleship (discipline) and love go hand-in-hand as much as the world abhors the thought of it and does everything to convince you otherwise.

Let me explain further with this from Theology of the Body by Christopher West:

"The tendency to 'grasp' seems built in to our fallen nature. We can observe it even in little children. For example, when my son asks for a cookie for dessert, before I can even get the cookie out of the box to present it to him as a gift, what does he do?

He grasps at it. Taking advantage of this teachable moment, I might say to my son, 'Hold on, you're denying the gift. Your papa loves you. I want to give this cookie to you as a gift. If you believed in the gift, all you would need to do is hold your hands out in confidence and receive the cookie as a gift.' This is the problem with us all. We do not trust enough in our Father's love, so we grasp at the 'cookie.'"

The Cookie Jar in Real Life – "Who'd You Buy the Roses For?"

I've known this gentleman most of my adult life and we are great friends. The Lord had brought us together again after several years of being caught up in our own marriages and family. He approached me one Sunday evening at church and asked if we could get together.

We spent some time catching up then he told me he'd had two marriages that had fallen apart.

This man still had some things to work through and lessons to learn as, after the second divorce, he quickly jumped back into another "rebound" relationship with a single mom. It was this relationship that helped us both learn more about God's kind of love.

After a few weeks of this couple dating and seeing each other nearly every day, she explained that the following week she would have to spend most of her time working and would not be able to see him. He understood, or so he thought.

On Tuesday evening of that week he decided to surprise her by stopping by her condo with a dozen roses. How romantic! He wished her well and let her know he was thinking of and praying for her.

On Friday evening he showed up fully expecting her to be ready to go out on another date as the week had passed and she was free, in his mind. But she had promised to spend that night with her daughter.

She was surprised to see him when she opened the door. There had been no communication on his part, simply expectation and assumption. She explained she'd reserved the evening for her daughter, and he said he understood and left.

When we met the next week he recounted the story of the week—the roses, the Friday night "rejection" and, as it had festered, he'd become quite agitated. He couldn't believe that she "stood him up" even though there was no date arranged.

We talked briefly about the communication side of things and he understood that his assumptions and expectations were guiding his emotional responses. He was still frustrated and said to me, "I can't believe after I left her alone all week—except for the roses and to tell her I was praying—that she would turn me down."

We'd been talking about relationship, love, communication, and expectations. I truly believe The Holy Spirit laid the next question on my mind, "Let me ask you one question."

"Sure," he said.

"Who'd you buy the roses for?" I asked.

"For her, of course," he retorted with a faint hint of disgust.

I repeated the question and he slowly and a little more thoughtfully repeated the same answer.

"I'll ask one more time," I said, "Who'd you really buy the roses for?"

He thought about it and it hit him. He looked at me and resignedly said, "I bought them for me, didn't I?"

"Now you're getting it. Friday night proved that Tuesday night you were being nice so you'd get something in return," I explained.

That's the culture's modus operandi when it comes to so-called love. But that's really lust because we do things with the full expectation of a return. God's love, agape, is selfless and reaches out and serves regardless of the response or return. It's hard to grasp in our selfish flesh, but the love He gives to us and desires for us to share with others never takes into consideration the expectations.

We will have expectations because we're human. The reality is that expectations are the termites of relationships. When we encounter unmet expectations we tend to define our partner, our relationships, and ourselves accordingly. I've seen this played out over and over whether it was roses, candy, gifts, sex or anything else from the cookie jar.

In God's design, we choose to give and love even when our expectations are not met. This is God's kind of love that He desires for us to have in every relationship, but we must remember that without Christ we can't love in this way. Self gets in the way every time.

CHAPTER 14

SELF & LUST: A MODERN DAY MOVIE/BIBLICAL STORY MASH-UP

The Boat & The Temptation

I present the Love & Lordship series multiple times a year. In our discussion on agape and porneia we view a clip from Fireproof: The Movie and connect it with King David's adultery with Bathsheba. A few years ago as I was presenting this The Holy Spirit gave me some insights that have helped many in their battle against porneia and other sins.

We view the clip where Caleb (Kirk Cameron's character) is looking at some pictures on his computer screen and up pops a porn invitation. He struggles with whether to click on it or not but chooses to read the "The Love Dare" journal that his father has challenged him to work through. He ultimately chooses against the porn and takes his computer monitor outside and destroys it with a baseball bat. It's both comical and poignant.

During one of these teaching sessions as we transitioned to talk about King David's struggles, I was prompted to ask if anyone noticed what Caleb was viewing on his computer when the "temptation" popped up? No one had noticed and neither had I for several years. He was viewing some really nice boats.

The backstory was that he was selfishly withholding things from his marriage and wife while saving money to buy a boat. Disclaimer: buying a boat is not in and of itself selfish, but for the purposes of the movie it clearly was. I then asked the men to explain the significance of what he was viewing. Silence. Here's the insight:

God has all foreknowledge and wisdom, which means He can see the future and know what we're thinking and our responses. Satan, on the other hand, does not have foreknowledge and can only respond and act on what we are thinking and choosing. This is why it's so important to guard our thoughts (2 Corinthians 10:5) and renew our minds (Romans 12:2) so he can't get a toe, foot or stronghold in our lives.

Isn't it interesting that as Caleb was viewing the boat, the item he was sure would fully satisfy him, the porn temptation popped up? The selfish state of his mind (in the movie it's clear the boat was an idol for him) made it easier for the enemy to draw him in. He chose to fight against it and won the battle.

Now let's apply that to King David. I'm going to fill in some gaps in the story to help us see how the self-absorbed mind makes it so much easier to fall into temptation and sin.

Second Samuel 11:1 says, "in the spring, at the time when kings go out to battle," and then proceeds to tell us that King David decided to send his general and army out to clean up some unfinished business in war while he lounged around his palace. There's nothing particularly sinful about his choice, but it does give us insight into his mind. He was thinking about David rather than his army.

The Bible gives no indication that he stayed home for any particular reason and especially not to look for naked women. One evening he's walking on his palace rooftop and sees a beautiful woman bathing. He's stricken with her and immediately asks his servant to inquire about her.

Here's where I interject David's potential and likely thought patterns based on his self-absorbed decision to stay home rather than go to battle with his men. What story do you think David may have crafted in his mind as his servant is inquiring about the beautiful woman?

Maybe it goes something like this..."I can't wait for my servant to return and tell me this woman's name and that she's single and available." This would align with God's commands.

The problem occurs when the servant returns to report that Bathsheba is not only married but it is to one of David's top men, Uriah the Hittite. Now David has to figure out if he's going to continue with the story in his mind where this woman is his to have or follow God's Truth and leave her to her husband.

Once again, the choice reveals where the mind is leading. David sends for her and sleeps with her. Seems like he's gotten away with it until Bathsheba sends a report that she's pregnant! It couldn't be her husband's baby as he's off fighting David's war.

David schemes to bring Uriah home so he'll sleep with his wife and cover it up. Uriah does the noble thing for both nights and does not sleep with his wife because that would not be right with the other warriors out to battle.

David improvises and sends a letter to Joab, commander of his army, to put Uriah on the front lines where the fighting is most fierce. As designed, Uriah is killed.

David then eventually marries Bathsheba and thinks the ruse is complete until the prophet Nathan approaches him approximately nine months later and tells him a story. While David recognizes the sin in the story, his sin has blinded him to the fact the he was the one guilty and deserving of death.

Here's what we need to learn from David and Caleb. We must guard our hearts and minds as self-absorbed thinking opens the door for the enemy to tempt us. The sooner we change our thinking, including at the very beginning as we dwell on our self, the easier it is to avoid the temptation. The more we think about self the easier it is to give in to the temptation, follow through on the sin, and even cover it up and be blind to it in our own eyes.

That's the nature of self, lust, pride, and sin, and the sooner we die to self and live for Christ and His love the stronger we are in Him to overcome any temptation.

Hesed/Agape – The Real Truth About Real Love

Let's spend the rest of this chapter on what God's Word has to say about love.

Don't miss this—God's love is a commitment, a choice, an act of the will. Feelings aside, we choose to love and, as a matter of Biblical principles, that's exactly what we're called to do in every relationship, whether it is our spouse, family member, or even an enemy. We make the choice to commit to what's best for them regardless of their actions or responses to us. We choose to guide our emotions, walking in Truth, rather than be guided by our feelings.

Love is also an intentional investment in others. We willingly submit and intentionally give of ourselves for their sake. We may not feel like it but we are always called, as disciples of Christ, to love—so we have to invest in others whether they choose to invest in us or not.

Can anyone say "Cookie Jar?"

CHAPTER 15

THE FULL-ORBED LOVE OF GOD

God's Love as Compassion

God's love is full-orbed—complete and multi-dimensional. Let me explain using the example of two men in Scripture and their personal encounter with Love Himself. With the first we find a love based on compassion that prompts the perfect response from Jesus. In Mark 1:40-42 (NKJV) "Now a leper came to Him, imploring Him, kneeling down to Him and saying to Him, 'If You are willing, You can make me clean.' Then Jesus, **moved with compassion,** stretched out His hand and touched him, and said to him, 'I am willing; be cleansed.' As soon as He had spoken, immediately the leprosy left him, and he was cleansed." (Emphasis added)

Here we see Jesus emotionally moved to compassion doing what any of us would expect—He healed Him. You don't even have to be a believer to like this guy. He heals people and restores their life and livelihood that leprosy, in this case, had stolen. What an act of love!

The Greek word *splanchnizomai* means to be moved with compassion or pity. This word and related words are used 12 other times in the New Testament and every time the word translates as someone being moved with emotion to the point of acting favorably for the other person.

I'm no Greek scholar, but it's very clear that Jesus' act of love was an act of compassion motivated by how He felt for the leper. I've never run across anyone who has a problem with what Jesus did. How loving and wonderful He was in His perfect love for the leper.

Before we move to the next man that Jesus encountered, let me offer a question to ponder: "Does God/Jesus always love perfectly?"

God's Love as Painful Truth

In Mark 10 Jesus is pursued by another young man. "As He was setting out on a journey, a man ran up to Him and knelt before Him, and asked Him, 'Good Teacher, what shall I do to inherit eternal life?' And Jesus said to him, 'Why do you call Me good? No one is good except God alone. You know the commandments, 'DO NOT MURDER, DO

NOT COMMIT ADULTERY, DO NOT STEAL, DO NOT BEAR FALSE WITNESS, DO NOT DEFRAUD, HONOR YOUR FATHER AND MOTHER.' And he said to Him, 'Teacher, I have kept all these things from my youth up.' Looking at him, **Jesus felt a love for him and said to him**, 'One thing you lack: go and sell all you possess and give to the poor, and you will have treasure in heaven; and come, follow Me.' But at these words he was saddened, and he went away grieving, for he was one who owned much property." (vv. 17-22 NASB, emphasis added)

I've heard dozens of sermons on the rich young ruler, and one thing I've never heard explained with any clarity was the phrase in verse 21: "Looking at him, Jesus felt a love for him." Fully believing that Jesus/ God always loved perfectly, I asked The Spirit to show me what's going on here. It's easy to see Christ's love for the leper, every one of us would have healed him had we the power.

The love for the rich young ruler that Jesus displayed is puzzling. If we're honest with ourselves as believers, and especially as modern-day church-going believers, we struggle with Jesus' response. Here the Greek word is *agapao*, rooted in agape or God's selfless, sacrificial love. Agapao is used 110 times and agape 106 times in the New Testament and every time it deals with love for others that esteems them above self—whether it is a family member, neighbor, stranger, or enemy.

What in the world is God trying to tell us? First of all, I think He is teaching us that His love expresses itself perfectly every time. In the case of these two men, one expression is with heartfelt compassion and the other in heart-spoken Truth. But I think there's a second thing that The Holy Spirit is trying to teach. The word defined as love with the rich young ruler is agapao and is stronger than love as compassion. While we must teach and model compassion, sharing truth is the most loving thing we can do and we must present it completely regardless of how those who hear it may respond. Jesus knew the rich young man would reject His loving truth, but the greatest and most perfect act of love was to tell Him the Truth that alone could set Him free. The feelings generated by love did not overrule the Truth that had to be expressed.

Some time after I'd prayed and come to this understanding, I was teaching these thoughts when a young man asked: "You've been talking about agape love as God's selfless, sacrificial love that He desires all of us to know in our marriages, families, and in His Church for each other and others. What was Jesus sacrificing in this case?"

Admittedly, I'd never gone that far; I'd just accepted what The Holy Spirit had shown me but this was a great question. I silently asked The Holy Spirit to guide me and here are the thoughts that immediately came to my mind that I shared with the group.

"You remember the guy who carried the money bag for Jesus and His apostles?" Several replied, "Judas." "Correct, and here's one way I think that Jesus was sacrificing. He could have said, 'Why don't you sell 90% or 50% or even 10% and put it in Judas' money bag? With your wealth we could really expand our ministry and reach many more.'" This in no way implies that Jesus desired this man's wealth or even to add another disciple to His growing number of followers. It simply gives an indication that Jesus love was much more about the truth that could set this man free than anything that might benefit Him and His ministry.

You see where I believe The Lord was leading me and teaching us? His love always begins in the heart of the individual involved. As we make more and more disciples and build relationships we expand our outreach and ministry through them. I want to be careful, but I'm not sure what else Jesus was sacrificing if it wasn't something that could be done for Him and His ministry. Yet He loved the man enough to tell him what he needed to hear even if it meant he would walk away—which is just what he did.

What does this mean as we learn about sacrifice and compassion when it comes to God's love toward us? How do we live in that love with Him and with others?

CHAPTER 16

GOD'S PRIORITIES

God makes it very obvious in His Word that there is a priority on love and relationships. He uses the words like "first" and "greatest," and that should compel us to respond with the same priority and urgency when it comes to love for Him and others.

Dr. Tony Evans wrote, "Our God is a Covenant-making and Covenant-keeping God and every Covenant has an order." So, what is the order of His Covenant? What are God's, and therefore our, priorities when it comes to relationships?

Priority of Relationships

The following precepts are what God has commanded, and encouraged with regard to living in relationship with Him and our fellow man (Scriptures for reference and study):

1) We love because He first loved us—we cannot know love apart from God. (1 John 4:19)
   Love must originate and be found in Him.

   In our love for Him and others we are actually given four commands summed up in the two greatest commands found first in Deuteronomy 6:4-5 and repeated in Mark 12:29-31 and Matthew 22:37-39. Notice the words "first," "greatest," and "second," as well as "all." He is literally giving us order and priority, which should carry over into all our relationships.

2) The First Command, Part 1–Honor and worship The Lord as The One and Only God. (Deuteronomy 6:4; Mark 12:29)

3) The First and Greatest Command, Part 2–Love the Lord with all you are. (Matthew 22:37-38; Mark 12:30)

4) Living the First Command–Seek The Lord and His Kingdom and righteousness first, above everything else in your life and with all your heart. (Jeremiah 29:11-13; Matthew 6:33)

5) The Second Command, Part 1–Love yourself—the self that God created you to be and recreated you to be in Christ (Matthew 22:39; Mark 12:31; Ephesians 2:10)—so you can die to yourself and complete the second command.

6) Second Command, Part 2–Love your neighbor (all others) as you love yourself, (Matthew 22:39; Mark 12:31) continuing with priority and order:

- Marriage – Only covenant/highest human relationship; as one in Christ this new "disciple" takes priority over either spouse (Matthew 19:4-6)

- Spouse – Reflects Christ and His Bride (Ephesians 5:21-27; 32-33)

- Children – God builds His family with Godly offspring (Malachi 2:13-16; Ephesians 6:4)

- Family members (I Timothy 3:5; 5:4, 8)

- Friends/Family of God (Galatians 6:10; 1 Peter 2:17); also remembering Christ's words regarding family (Luke 8:20-22)

- Others/Worldly Acquaintances (Romans 12:18, 21; Galatians 6:10)

- Enemies (Matthew 5:11, 44; Luke 10:30-37; Romans 12:14)

Here's the power of what God has given us in prioritizing how we are to love:

Priorities reveal who is Lord/lord in our life. Priorities also order our decision-making and our relationships. Our time and schedules should reflect this. We can order our thoughts, lives, and decisions to show the love we are given and called to share in a way that brings us His Shalom or wholeness and peace.

We will have to sacrifice; that is what love does. This is how we are to build relationships together as His disciples to grow His Church and His Kingdom.

Here is one final note in tying together discipleship and relationship. If discipleship is lived out in relationship and relationships are formed and matured through loving discipleship, then we should follow God's Covenant Order when it comes to discipling believers in Christ.

Leaders, how often do we place, implicitly or explicitly, the needs of the local fellowship and community above that of personal maturity in Christ and marriages and families within the church? How often have we encouraged, cajoled, and even manipulated members to sign up and serve, having spent little or no time discipling them in the greatest commands...worship and love God first, know and love who we are in Christ?

Church members, have you ever felt pushed to serve, or manipulated into service for others while still very young in Christ? Did you have any idea what it meant to know and love Him with your whole being and love who you are in Him so you could truly love others?

When have we discipled, in a deep and ongoing way, new and young believers in what it means to know, worship, and love God with all they are? When have we discipled them to understand that they are deeply loved and as they come to know, worship, and love God with their whole being, He will show them who they are in Christ so they can love themselves?

Only then can we, by following God's priorities and order for relationships, begin to see disciples who can love their neighbors as they love themselves. Finally we can and must love as Christ did by giving ourselves away for others.

The world will see the difference in our relationships and our service. Then we can build loving relationships that are His Church and can impact the culture and world for His Kingdom!

The Rest of the Story

Back to the story that opened this section.

Following the prompting of the Holy Spirit, I said to the group: "One more question, and please don't raise your hand on this one. How many of you are going to the PK conference just so you don't have to spend time with your spouse and family?"

You could hear a pin drop, and many heads did as well.

After we were dismissed several men (every one that speaks up represents ten that are afraid to) came up to me and said words to this effect: "You nailed me. It sounds really good to attend a Christian men's conference and claim to be a Christ follower, but I'm not doing it where it really counts, with my wife and children."

We love attending events, conferences and men's breakfasts, etc., in order to claim that we are, or are becoming, Godly men. But when it comes to stepping up and fulfilling the actual role of being Godly husbands, fathers, and disciples as His Word tells us, we tend to fall short of the mark.

This is not a condemnation of PK or other excellent groups calling men to this standard. I believe they would agree with my line of questioning and peeling back the layers to expose the real issues that

God is calling us to as men, husbands and fathers, as disciples! And the same holds true for the women of God.

> *"To be faithful in every circumstance means that we have only one loyalty, and that is to our Lord...We will be loyal to work, to service, to anything, but do not ask us to be loyal to Jesus Christ...The idea is not that we do work for God, but that we are so loyal to Him that He can do His work throug us — "I reckon on you for extreme service, with no complaining on your part and no explanation on Mine." God wants to use us as He used His own Son."*

— Oswald Chambers, *My Utmost for His Highest*

STUDY GUIDE
RELATIONSHIPS: WHAT WE WERE CREATED FOR

Key Concepts

1) Discipleship is lived out in Relationship, with Christ and others.

2) Loving relationships are the currency of Christ's Kingdom.

3) Either people or things will be sacrificed, depending on whether we are building relationships for His Kingdom or for ourselves.

4) Lusts of the flesh and the eye, and pride of the mind all destroy relationships.

5) Porneia is the greatest destroyer of loving relationships as it is the greatest expression of lust.

6) Hesed/Agape is the sacrificial, selfless love of God that is freely given to us and allows us to love in return.

7) Agape and porneia (or any pride/lust) cannot coexist. The one you willingly submit to will eventually win out in your heart.

8) The Cookie Jar is an analogy of discipline, relationship, love and lust.

9) Love is a commitment, a choice, and an act of our will lived out in intentional investment in the lives of others.

10) God's love is a full-orbed love as seen in healing the leper and speaking tough Truth to the rich young ruler.

11) God's love is lived out according to His Covenant Order in the priorities of relationships.

Questions

1) How does your discipleship relationship affect all other relationships?

2) How do you see relationships as the currency in Christ's Kingdom?

3) How are you sacrificing things for relationships? Relationships for things?

4) What do you see in your life that is helping grow your relationships?

5) What is hindering or harming your relationships?

6) Are you involved in porneia? If so, do you have an accountability partner (someone to disciple you in your relationship with The Lord and with others)?

7) What do your decisions say about how you're prioritizing your relationships?

8) Are you discipling anyone in their relationship with The Lord and others?

Discussion

1) How do you think your discipleship affects your relationships? How do your relationships help or hinder your walk with The Lord?

2) Do the stories of Christ's perfect love toward the leper and rich young ruler help you understand His love or muddy the waters?

3) Where would your spouse say you rate him/her in the priority of relationships? Your children? The Church?

Action Item

Find (or form) a small group with the focus of growing together in Christ and holding each other accountable.

SECTION 5

MARRIAGE: IN GOD'S IMAGE

"So they called Rebekah and asked her,
"Will you go with this man?"
"I will go," she said. (Genesis 24:58)

"And she said, 'I will go.' Those words are the answer to
Eliezer's prayer. Rebekah felt the thrill which always passes
through any pure young heart in the presence of a saint. A
soul's trust in a saint in the providence of God is something
more precious even than love. Few of us know anything about
this because we are too sordidly selfish; we want things for
ourselves all the time. Eliezer had only one conception, loyalty
to his master, and in the providence of God he brought Rebekah
straight to Isaac. ***This marriage, like all true marriages,***
concerns the Kingdom of God."

— Oswald Chambers, *My Utmost for His Highest*
(emphasis added)

The Highest of Human Relationships

We've established the Biblical priorities of relationship beginning with Christ as Lord and our worship and love for Him above all else if we are to walk as His disciples. Looking further at Scripture we recognize that the priorities continue in our earthly relationships, recognizing that marriage is the highest of human relationships.

You may have heard a pastor call The Bible "the greatest love letter ever written." I would propose that we take that a step further and declare it the "greatest marriage manual ever written!" This is for many reasons, including: the Creation design itself of male and female; the image of God reflected in the differences and the union; and the concept of Covenant ordained by God through marriage as the relationship that symbolizes His covenant with His people Israel, Christ and His Bride, The Church, and the marriage of one man and one woman in a lifetime commitment. Every single word in Scripture is written to one, two, or all three of the following: His Bride, Israel; Christ's Bride, The Church; and one man/one woman in covenant marriage.

The question in our world and churches today: Are we giving marriage its proper place and honor? I argue that we are not, and both The Church and our culture are suffering greatly as a result.

CHAPTER 17

MARRIAGE IS THE #2 PRIORITY

Marriage should be esteemed, second only to Christ, above every other relationship and institution in our culture, including The Church, as it preceded and is implicitly and explicitly given such honor in Scripture. This was driven home to me several times early in my marriage.

I had several opportunities to pursue a professional basketball career, either in the U.S. or abroad. In submitting to The Lord, I chose a different path, and this was all prior to even meeting my wife. I continued to play with a couple of traveling teams that allowed me to keep my skills sharpened and my competitive appetite whetted. This also kept my name as a potential player in the loop.

I met Ami in 1988 and we dated for nearly two years, were engaged for exactly one year, and married June 1, 1991. I was teaching and coaching at the time and continued to play competitively. She became pregnant with our firstborn, Lansing, in 1995 and just a couple of months prior to his birth I received a call from a top-level team in Switzerland about a position as a player/coach. Again in 1997, just five days before our second son, Harrison, was born, I received the same offer from a top club team in London.

In my flesh, I really would have loved to pursue these offers. However, I'd made up my mind entering into marriage that my first priority would be The Lord, my marriage would be next, and then my wife and family. My understanding of Scripture was that the priorities that had come from His Word were to guide my decisions.

I knew that my "hooping" all over Switzerland or England and beyond while my wife managed two toddler boys would have been very difficult for our marriage and family.

The decisions were easy. I humbly and politely declined both offers and I've never regretted it. What I can tell you is that God has blessed our marriage and family and I believe it was because I kept my priorities in line with His Word and placed Him, and my marriage, wife, and family above myself.

A few years later two similar situations occurred just a few years apart. I was asked to be a national spokesperson for an expanding nonprofit. At the time, our three children (we added our beautiful daughter,

Haidyn, in 1999) were elementary age or younger. My response was simple: "How can I help raise my children if I'm traveling all over the country?" The founder and CEO replied, "I thought you might say that, but we had to try anyway."

The second inquiry for the same position came a few years later with Lansing just entering middle school and Harrison and Haidyn in elementary school. This time they asked: "Did you know that you could fly to two-thirds of the continental U.S. and back home in a day?" As much as I would have enjoyed that position and Ami and I would have loved to travel around the country, my answer again reflected the priorities that had guided me in my walk with The Lord. I responded with a question: "How does leaving at 6 a.m. and arriving back home at 9 p.m. or later honor my marriage and wife or help raise my children?"

I closed that conversation with this simple statement of faith: "If The Lord desires me to be in that or any similar position, then He will show me the time and place. And if not, then I'm fine with what I've chosen."

Please know I'm not condemning anyone who has made or may make a different choice. I'm simply sharing with you why I made the choices based on my understanding of God's Covenant Order and how He has blessed us in our marriage and family. I would not trade that for anything.

I can tell you that I have counseled hundreds who have made different decisions in similar situations and have sat in my office with great regret for what they sacrificed.

Remember, relationships in the Kingdom, or the stuff of this world: at some point one or the other will be sacrificed. Your choices and actions determine which is sacrificed no matter how you may claim, "I did it for my family."

Marriage Should Be Honored By All

Most Bible scholars would agree that Hebrews and Romans are the two deepest theological letters in all of Scripture. I find it very interesting that near the end of Hebrews, we find this verse, "Marriage should be honored by all, and the marriage bed kept pure, for God will judge the adulterer and all the sexually immoral." (Hebrews 13:4)

All means all, right? So The Holy Spirit is not just saying that all those who are married, have been married, or are planning on getting married, should honor marriage. All means all!

Why is this important? Simple. God had a perfect design from the beginning and the only way we can honor it is if we are willing to walk according to His design for relationships, sexuality, marriage, and family.

This doesn't mean that everyone has to get married. It does mean that everyone is to honor marriage. Simply put, sex is reserved for marriage, period. All other sexual activity is sin. This includes promiscuity or fornication (sex before/outside of marriage), cohabitation, adultery, pornography, lust (Matthew 5:27-28), polygamy, homosexuality, transgenderism, bestiality, and pedophilia, to name a few among the ever-increasing depravity of our sexual culture.

There are grave consequences personally, relationally, socially, and even eternally in God's judgment of the sexually immoral, as evident in our pornified culture today.

But there is also grace and forgiveness. As with any other sin, forgiveness is free in Christ but it is not to be abused and mocked.

Honoring marriage begins long before you say, "I do," and extends throughout marriage and beyond. God's truth about honoring marriage is about honoring His creation in relationships, sexuality, marriage, and family.

Our Creator God began everything with a relationship of love known as marriage. This is the closest we can come in human experience to His agape love and it must be done in covenant commitment. Relationships are His design for living out His love in His image in covenant marriage between one man and one woman, through family and friends, and even loving our enemies. It's all in line with His sacrificial, selfless kind of love—AGAPE!

Allow me to tie all of this together as we move from Lordship, discipleship, and relationship to unpack all that God has packed into marriage.

First and foremost, we must understand that the perfect model for marriage is Christ and His Bride, The Church. Ephesians 5:25-57, 31-32 make this clear, "Husbands, love your wives, just as Christ loved the church and gave himself up for her to make her holy, cleansing her by the washing with water through the word, and to present her to himself as a radiant church, without stain or wrinkle or any other blemish, but holy and blameless...'For this reason a man will leave his father and mother and be united to his wife, and the two will become one flesh.' This is a profound mystery—but I am talking about Christ and the church."

God has shown us how much He values marriage in His design and highest desire for its sanctity, His command that all should honor it, and its reflection of His image and our relationship with Him. We would be wise to take this responsibility with all the weight that He intends for it to have in His design and purpose for marriage.

The goal of every relationship is to imitate Christ. The only way we can do this is if He is our Lord. That makes discipleship the key to every good relationship and especially the most important earthly one—marriage.

Are you content to place other worldly relationships ahead of your marriage? Or are you making it the priority as God sees it? You will be blessed if you do.

With this in mind let's connect the dots with regard to His Lordship, our discipleship relationship with Him, and all loving relationships, finding the highest expression in the marriage relationship.

CHAPTER 18

BUILDING AGAPE MARRIAGES & KINGDOM RELATIONSHIPS

God has given us this very clear blueprint on how we are to build relationships with and in Him. There is a priority order made possible only because He first loved us (1 John 4:19).

Please understand that if you don't get anything else from this book...DON'T MISS THIS. It will literally change your life and every relationship for the better if you will follow through with this understanding in line with His Word.

In giving the greatest commands (Matthew 22:37-39; Mark 12:29-31) Jesus was not giving them in priority simply because God is most important. That is true, but there is something else in the original language that makes all the difference in understanding who we are and how we can most fully and freely live out our lives and relationships.

We cannot live out these commands in relationships in any other order. No matter how we try we cannot love others until we have learned to love ourselves. And we cannot love ourselves until we first love God and allow Him to show us who we are recreated to be in Christ. This is a lifelong process of maturing as Christ's disciple.

With this understanding, here are the three commands and keys to building agape Kingdom relationships, especially marriages and families, according to His Word.

1) Worship God alone and love Him with all you are! (Deuteronomy 6:4-6; Mark 12:29-30) If we do not spend time to get to know, worship and love Him, we will struggle in every other relationship.

   Submission is the key found in what we are called to do in honoring one another in relationships and particularly in marriage. Ephesians 5:21-25: "Submit to one another out of reverence for Christ. Wives, submit yourselves to your own husbands as you do to the Lord. For the husband is the head of the wife as Christ is the head of the church, his body, of which he is the Savior. Now as the church submits to Christ, so also wives should submit to their husbands in everything. Husbands, love your wives, just as Christ loved the church and gave himself up for her."

Wives are commanded to submit to their husbands. This is not a command to the husband to make his wife submit but to the wife to willingly choose to submit to her husband because she has already submitted to Christ.

A husband is called to submit in love and servant-leadership, literally to submit or surrender his life for his wife just as Christ did for The Church. Again, wives, this is not a command to you to make your husband love you. This is a command to we husbands to be obedient to Christ by daily choosing to love our wife because we have first submitted to Christ and learned to love God.

Years ago The Spirit revealed one of the most profound teachings and I have taught it faithfully ever since. It has changed countless husbands and, in the process, marriages (and wives) for His glory.

Remember every marriage is intended to reflect His image and glorify Him and also, husbands, that we are the Christ figure in our marriage!

In my prayer and study, I was challenged to go beyond the obvious question, "Husbands, would you take a bullet (die) for your wife?" This is a question most pastors, Christian counselors, or marriage therapists ask, reiterating to husbands the command "to love their wife and give up their life for her as Christ did the Church." As I thought through this The Spirit took me to Philippians 2:5-8. I didn't get it at first, but the more I prayed and meditated it became clear.

The Apostle Paul, who wrote both Ephesians and Philippians, was giving instructions to husbands as to what it truly cost Christ to "lay down His life for His Bride." Our first love has to be our love for God. It is from His love for us, and our growing in our love for Him, that we can love all others, leading to our second command and key.

2) Love Who You Are in Christ! (Matthew 22:39: Mark 12:31) What is true in every other relationship is even more impactful in marriage. As we mature in our love for God, loving Him with our whole self, He is able to reveal more and more to us who we are created, and recreated in Christ, to be. Only then can we learn to truly love who we are. Remember this is the essence of our second key:

Humility—Philippians 2:3-8 "Do nothing out of selfish ambition or vain conceit. Rather, **in humility** value others above yourselves, not looking to your own interests but each of you to the interests of the others. In your relationships with one another, **have the same mindset as Christ Jesus**: Who, being in very nature God, did not consider equality with God something to be used to his own advantage; rather, **he made himself nothing** by taking the very nature of a servant, being made in human likeness. And being found in appearance as a man, **he humbled himself** by becoming obedient to death—even death on a cross!" (Emphasis added)

As we allow God to reveal who we are in Christ we begin to form Christ's Mind in us. The description of Christ shows a character of humility—knowing and being confident and content of who we are in Christ so we can place others above ourselves.

Imagine what our marriages and all relationships would look like as we practice humility in Christ!

Now that we've read through what Christ did for His Bride we can understand and apply Paul's teaching from Ephesians more fully when it comes to "laying down our life for our wife."

Christ did more than just give up His physical life. The passage above describes in detail that the first thing Jesus gave up was His lifestyle—all the glorious life He had with The Father in heaven.

Think about it. When Paul writes that we are to lay down our lives just as Christ did for His Bride, he fully understood that we husbands would need to lay down our lifestyles and place the needs and desires of our wife above our own. This has to hold true because had Jesus not surrendered His life style in heaven first, then He could not have become fully God and fully man and His death on The Cross (what we always equate with "giving up our life for our wife") would have meant nothing.

I know it's not easy, but it's good because it is what He has called us to and He did nothing less than model it for us!

Now we are beginning to grasp what love truly is and how we can love our wife, family, and all others, which is our third command and key.

3) Love Others As You Love Yourself! (Matthew 22:39; Mark 12:31) We cannot fully love others unless we have first begun to grow in our love for God and for ourselves. This should be paramount in how we make disciples. Teach and train first to love God, and love who we are in Christ so we can then love others and show them His love, bringing us to the third key:

Servant's Heart—we see this when Jesus washes His disciples' feet and then instructs them to do the same for others in John 13:12-17. "When he had finished washing their feet, he put on his robe and returned to his place. 'Do you understand what I have done for you?' he asked them. 'You call me 'Teacher' and 'Lord,' and rightly so, for that is what I am. Now that I, your Lord and Teacher, have washed your feet, you also should wash one another's feet. I have set you an example that you should do as I have done for you. Very truly I tell you, no servant is greater than his master, nor is a messenger greater than the one who sent him. Now that you know these things, you will be blessed if you do them.'"

This is the culmination where love (v.1), humility (v.3), serving (vv.4-5), authority (v.13) and now discipleship (vv. 14-17) come together. This is what Kingdom relationships are to look like...and the highest of those is Marriage.

"Christ's idea is that we serve Him by being the servants of other men...He says that in His Kingdom he that is greatest shall be the servant of all. The real test of the saint is not preaching the gospel, but washing disciples' feet, that is, doing the things that do not count in the actual estimate of men but count everything in the estimate of God."

— Oswald Chambers, *My Utmost for Highest*

Imagine once again what our marriages, families and churches would look like if we made disciples that loved God above everything else, loved who we are in Christ and loved one another as Christ loved us. Marriage and family should be integral to His Church, not just going to Church!

This is Christ in us and through us, as we love others in His Covenant Order:

Marriage ⇨ Spouse ⇨ Children and Family ⇨ His Church ⇨ The World

94

King Arthur is credited with saying, "In serving each other we become free." This is the truth for every disciple of Christ and in every marriage, family, and relationship as we build the currency of His Kingdom.

May He find us faithful as His disciples to love as He loved us—this is how the world can see Who He is through us and come to know Him. May it begin in your marriage (and in mine) and may our families and churches be blessed as we live and love in His Truth!

I learned this early in our marriage. Ami came from a divorced family and, as is very common, there are deep issues of trust and distrust. We discussed this often and prayed and worked diligently to both be aware of the issues and circumstances that would trigger distrust as well as those that would build trust.

About three years into our marriage, she called one evening as I was in my office late. My job was athletic director and head basketball coach with a small private Christian school that owned none of the fields, gyms, or facilities that we used to practice and compete. At any moment we could lose use of a facility and the schedule would need to be reworked. That meant making calls to the schools we were competing against, referees, and parents.

Fairly often I worked late to set up the schedule for the next day.

One night Ami called and I could hear the pain in her voice. She explained what we'd talked about many times before, that whenever I didn't show up at or near the appointed time, distrust would rear its ugly head. This happened too many times as I got caught up in getting things in order.

She said, "If you would just give me a call and let me know what's going on and reassure me that all is well, it would help me a lot."

As I've shared this with many men and couples, the typical prideful male response is, "She's just checking up on me and I don't need another Momma! She just needs to trust me." Knowing I was doing nothing wrong or worthy of distrust, I had entertained the same thoughts.

However, before I said anything, I said a quick prayer and in that moment The Holy Spirit simply prompted me to think, "Pride or humility? Your choice."

I asked Ami what she needed and she said, "If you'd just call once or twice a day, especially if something happens and you know your schedule is going to change, that would help me so much."

Simple, right? I either tell her to get over it and trust me, or I do something to help her build more trust in me. The Holy Spirit's prompting came to me again and it really was simple. Pride would put the burden on her and continue to lead to distrust. Humility put the burden on me to do all I could to show her that she could trust me.

I began the next day and have not missed a day of calling or texting her in the 26-plus years since. Distrust faded and trust became her default as God directed me to think of her above myself and I obeyed instead of giving into my pride. With that trust came an ever-growing peace in our marriage and family. Totally worth it!

I close this with what I share with every guy that I counsel on this: "You can choose to think, 'I don't need another Momma,' or you can humbly do what's best for your wife and marriage. Two to four minutes of calls or texts each day will mean two to four hours of peace each evening, and more over the course of your marriage, as long as you are honest and trustworthy. Or you can choose to put the burden on her and watch the tension and distrust build each evening and throughout your marriage. Seems like a 'no-brainer' to me, but it's your choice."

CHAPTER 19

BIBLICAL TIPS FOR NAVIGATING MARRIAGE

There are volumes that address most of the "how to's" in marriage. The purpose of this book, and this chapter in particular, is to help us make sure that our hearts and minds are aligned with Christ's. While there are practical steps in this book, if our hearts are not set on Him we will eventually just exchange one selfish desire for another and the enemy will wreak havoc in our life, marriage, and all relationships.

I know your desire is to honor God or you wouldn't be reading this book.

With this understanding let's take a look at a few more Scriptural principles that will reveal and/or help us deal with some of the underlying and prevalent issues and problems that arise in marriage. Using the foundations, commands, and keys previously discussed we can apply His Word and begin to see how He changes our hearts and guides us through them.

Authority in Marriage

Having already discussed this throughout this book, I simply want to give you a couple of acronyms to help you remember what authority in Christ's Kingdom, and therefore in our lives and marriage as His followers, is to look like. You need two pairs of P.A.N.T.S. to succeed in marriage, and they're really the same pair.

P.A.N.T.S.
Proper Authority Needed To Succeed
and
Proper Attitude Needed To Serve

Remember you're not wearing the first pair
if you're not willing to wear the second.

A Marriage Parody on Loving Servant-Leadership

In the Love & Lordship events I share this parody but before I do I remind husbands and wives that it may not be a clothes basket in their home so just fill in the blank with your issue.

Clothes Basket on the Stairs

A couple has been married about five years. The husband comes home from work and as he ascends the steps he sees a clothes basket. He wonders to himself, "What in the world is that?"

He walks on up the stairs and gets ready for the evening.

About four years later he encounters the basket on the stairs again. This time he thinks, "That's a clothes basket. Somebody's doing laundry."

Another three years pass and he comes home and finds the clothes basket once again on the stairs. "This must be my wife doing these clothes. She's really good as this is the third time in 12 years that she's done the laundry." So he shouts up the steps, "Honey, thanks for doing the laundry."

Now it's been nearly 13 years and he comes home one evening to an empty house. He again sees the basket full of clean clothes on the stairs and thinks, "Wow, my wife is incredible. She's done laundry four times in 13 years!"

He decides to put the clothes away himself. His wife comes in after carting the kids around to piano, soccer, drama and karate practice on top of the long day of cleaning and yes, the clothes. She drops into bed and immediately falls asleep giving no thought to the missing clothes basket.

All is well until the next morning when fireworks explode as no one can find their clothes. Shirts are where pants should be. Pants are in with underwear. Bras are with blouses and everyone is running late.

When I finish this parody, I ask the wives what it would mean for their husband to be involved in such a way that there would be no fireworks? Usual answers include, "It means he cares" or, "it means he loves us."

Then I ask them "Why?" Most have to think about this. I then add, "It means he's invested in you, your marriage, and your family. He takes the time to know you and that's what love does and is."

Don't dismiss this story because clothes and laundry aren't your issue: fill in the blank with an area where you are neglectful or unwilling to serve and begin today to change that. You will be amazed at what it does in your marriage if you both are willing to intentionally invest in each other and your marriage.

I shared this quote with a young man I was mentoring who was later called into the ministry. "Time, not money, is the real currency of our lives. Money, when spent, can be replenished. Time, when spent, is gone forever." – R. Triplett

He called me one evening, saying he was very busy studying for his ministry class and was going to have to back out of date night with his wife. I shared the quote and my thoughts about living out the priorities of relationships in the correct order. He said he had assured his wife that "his heart was with her."

I quoted Matthew 6:21 replacing the word "treasure" with perhaps the greatest treasures that God gives us: time and our spouse. I reminded him that whatever he spends his time doing is where his heart ultimately is. So he was only deceiving himself when he chose to miss date night but soften the blow to his wife by saying his heart was with her.

He promptly stopped his studying and went on a date with his wife. He also finished the class, went into a fruitful campus ministry position, and now he and his wife are working together in a successful real estate venture. God is good and if we will heed His words and wisdom, regardless of the cost, we will be blessed.

Forgiveness & Trust

In almost every case with struggling couples, no matter what the symptoms are, there are major foundational issues rooted in unforgiveness and distrust. I want to share some Scripture and insights that have helped many.

Forgiveness is mandatory (Matthew 6:14-15; Ephesians 4:32); Trust is earned. (John 2:24)

I tweeted some time ago, "God's grace is amazing, but it never compromises His Truth."

Unfortunately, we have compromised His Truth. Many in counseling settings have fallen into this trap.

Numerous couples have been told that forgiveness is a process and they would not be able to forgive until they had "processed" the pain and moved beyond the emotions, hurt feelings and accusations. Stay with me here.

There is a process. It's just that forgiveness is not that process. Emotions and feelings associated with the offense or violation do require time and processing. Forgiveness, on the other hand, is a choice that you can make immediately because it's what God has done for each of us who believe in Christ. According to His Word, forgiveness is a mandate—a command (Ephesians 4:32). The only thing that Jesus repeated after "The Lord's Prayer" (Matthew 6:9-13) is forgiveness (vv. 14-15). If you do not forgive, then your Heavenly Father will not forgive you. If I want to know His forgiveness, then I must forgive everyone, period.

This is the subtle deception that has entered into our counseling and wreaked havoc on countless marriages, families and relationships. If I'm not ready (i.e., don't feel like it), then I should allow time to "process" my feelings before I forgive. This ties forgiveness to our feelings rather than His Truth. I don't see that concept in God's Word. Again, His grace is amazing, but it never compromises His Truth.

If you allow feelings to trump God's Truth, then you give the enemy territory and ammunition. He will use your flesh through your emotions to steal, kill, and destroy you and others in the struggle and process. It's not a good ride or a gentle landing.

On the other hand, this Truth has helped many couples and people: If you are obedient to God to forgive, choosing to do so by His grace in and through you, then His Spirit and Truth will guide you through the emotional pain and process.

Know you are now forgiven and free in Christ as you give the same to others!

While forgiveness is tied directly to trust they are not the same. If we are willing to forgive, then we can rebuild trust but it takes time. Even Jesus did not trust others because He knew what was in their heart. (John 2:24) In less than three years, because He had taught and modeled truth, love and forgiveness for them, Jesus entrusted His life story, The Gospel, to 120 men and women in an upper room (Acts 2:1-4). His forgiveness had allowed His life to be formed in them and that is what He was trusting.

We can do the same in our marriage and in all relationships, including in His Church, if we are willing to walk as His disciples, forgive others, learn to live as He did, and begin to see His life in them.

Unconditional Love & Marriage

Marriage is based on Commitment and Unconditional Love. Here's a simple and great definition for love, based on Christ's for His Bride demonstrated on The Cross: Give 100%, Expect 0%! Maybe I should say "Demand 0."

Expectations and demands will naturally occur in our flesh. The issue is how you'll respond and how you'll define your spouse, yourself, and your relationship based on unmet expectations. We will all experience expectations—and unmet expectations—in our lives and marriage. The trouble comes when we play God and demand that our expectations always be met.

Learn to love and serve even when the expectations are not met. Not only will more of them be realized over time, but also you will become the person who is more interested in looking to meet your spouse's needs rather than always expecting your spouse to meet yours.

CHAPTER 20

TOUCHING THE HOT TOPICS

God's Word on Marriage, Adultery, Divorce & Remarriage

I want to close this section on marriage with what God has to say about adultery, divorce and remarriage.

As I've prayed and studied, here is where The Lord has led me with regard to these controversial issues:

1) God ordained marriage to reflect His Image and to be in lifetime covenant. (Genesis 2:24; Matthew 19:5-6)

2) Marriage reflects the relationship between God and Israel, and Christ and His Bride, the Church. (Jeremiah 31:31-32; Ephesians 5:25-27)

3) God hates divorce and the breaking of the covenant. (Malachi 2:16)

4) There are many reasons Moses permitted divorce, all found in the "hardness of our hearts." Marriage requires serious forethought before entering into it. (Matthew 19:7-10)

5) There is NO Scriptural basis for remarriage after divorce, although there are two concerns subject to Scriptural interpretation:
   - Marital unfaithfulness/sexual infidelity (Matthew 19:9);
   - Unbelieving spouse leaves the marriage (1 Corinthians 7:10-16)

6) One allowance for remarriage is death of spouse. (1 Corinthians 7:39) All other remarriage ends in adultery for both spouses upon remarriage. (Mark 10:11; Luke 16:18)

7) Divorce and remarriage—not unpardonable sin. (Only one is blasphemy or rejection of Holy Spirit received only through Christ) (Matthew 12:31)

I was invited to share the Love & Lordship message at an International Marriage and Family Conference in Cameroon, West Africa. The Holy Spirit made it clear that I was to go and shortly after confirmed it for Ami.

We made all our plans for travel and childcare, got our shots and passports, and took off for Cameroon in November 2010. We had a wonderful week and over 1,100 people attended.

We closed out on a Thursday night and I taught on the information laid out above on marriage, divorce, remarriage and adultery.

We ended the week with a pastors' conference on Saturday. Approximately 50 pastors and spouses showed up and I spoke about taking the message to a lost and hurting world.

As we wrapped up the pastors' conference and the week, the gentleman who had been our chauffeur and my interpreter approached me. I could see he was moved as he took my hand and began to speak with tears in his eyes and a lump in his throat.

He said, "I want to thank you for coming to Cameroon and speaking God's Truth to us. My wife and I were set free on Thursday night after God's message through you. We've never had an American pastor speak it so plainly, graciously and boldly."

Needless to say, I was both encouraged and disheartened. Encouraged personally, but disheartened by the reality that tough issues are often ignored or soft-pedaled.

He went on to share that he went home and told his wife that he needed to pray with her and ask her forgiveness. She asked him why and he said, "I now know that I've committed adultery" because his first wife had left him and he had now married her, his second wife.

They knelt and prayed for over an hour. When they stood up with tears in their eyes they looked at each other and said, "I feel like a weight has just been lifted from our shoulders and we can now truly become one and do all that God has called us to do."

He thanked me again and left as I stood there, tears now filling my eyes.

Everyone else had left except for the pastor who had invited us and coordinated the entire conference. He approached me and asked if the interpreter had shared his story with me. I said he had and how awesome it was to see God show up in that way.

The pastor asked, "Do you know who he is? " I answered, in a matter of fact tone, "He's the chauffeur and interpreter."

He said, "He is the president of the entire Western African Association of Churches. Did you see...?"

Before he could finish I said, "All week long all the other pastors had kept him literally at arm's length with short, curt greetings and stiff handshakes. Everyone else was greeted with deep heartfelt hugs. Today every single pastor and their wife gave him a hearty and long hug."

The pastor said that since his divorce and remarriage, the founding church in the U.S. made it clear that he would remain as president but everyone, including himself, struggled with the issues of remarriage and adultery until I taught on Thursday night.

"We've had great difficulty coming together as a church in our country but today that all changed."

I replied, as I had to the interpreter (president) when he shared that he and his wife knew they had been set free on Thursday night, "That's what happens when God's Truth is taught and received. People, couples and even churches are set free."

I pray that you will receive all of the teachings from God's Word throughout this book and test them to see if they are of Him and therefore true. If so, I pray that you follow them with all your heart in every relationship, especially in your marriage and family and in His Church.

Only when the sanctity of Marriage and Family under the Lordship of Christ and according to the Truth of Scripture has been restored will we see true revival and servant-leadership in the Church and Godly influence and impact in the culture rather than the other way around... the culture influencing our churches.

Only when the sanctity of Marriage and Family under the Lordship of Christ and according to the Truth of Scripture has been restored will we see true revival and servant-leadership in the Church and then Godly influence and impact in the culture rather than the other way around...the culture influencing our churches.

STUDY GUIDE
MARRIAGE: IN GOD'S IMAGE

Key Concepts

1) In God's design, every marriage is a covenant, making it the most important of all human relationships.

2) Marriage is the union of differences. Communication is at the core of Unity.

3) God's design for the marriage covenant is a lifetime commitment.

4) Two pairs of P.A.N.T.S. essential for Marriage.

   - Proper Authority Needed To Succeed
   - Proper Attitude Needed To Serve

5) Marriage always reflects on Christ and His Bride, The Church, and on His Gospel.

6) Three Keys to Agape Marriage: 1) Submission; 2) Humility; 3) Servant's Heart.

7) Forgiveness is mandatory. Trust is earned. These go together but they are not the same thing.

8) Unconditional (Agape) Love = Give 100%; Expect 0! Don't let unmet expectations define you, your spouse or your relationship.

   9) Meeting each other's needs requires daily dying to self through communication and submission in humility, integrity, and purity.

Key Questions

1) What is the connection between Love and Respect, service and authority?

2) How can you practice building great relationships and an "agape marriage"?

3) What does unconditional mean? What's the closest you've come to experiencing unconditional love/respect? What's the best you've done in giving it?

4) Why is forgiveness so important? Why is Trust so important?

5) What does it take to really meet someone else's needs?

Discussion

1) What's the most difficult obstacle you've found to building a lasting relationship?

2) Where are you when it comes to forgiveness and trust in your marriage or in any relationship?

3) Talk about the connection between love, humility, serving and authority.

4) Talk about marriage...your thoughts, ideas, experiences... good and bad.

Action Items

Today, take time to write down any bitterness or unforgiveness that you've held on to. Write down issue(s) and names. Begin with your spouse. Pray and ask God to forgive you for your disobedience. Then ask Him to give you the strength to specifically forgive each person and situation and to ask for forgiveness.

Marriage Activity – this will bless your marriage (do it at least once annually)

Willard Harley in his book, *His Needs, Her Needs*, lists the top 10 needs, by gender, in Marriage based on 30,000 couples over 25 years.

<u>Women</u>	<u>Men</u>
1) Affection (read Love)	1) Sexual Fulfillment (read Sex)
2) Conversation	2) Recreational Companionship
3) Honesty and Openness	3) Attractive Spouse
4) Financial Support	4) Domestic Support
5) Family Commitment	5) Admiration (read Respect)

Dr. Harley's list gives you an idea. Your list may be similar or quite different but in my experience the lists are usually comparable to his. Here's the activity...

1. Individually rank and personally define your needs.

2. List ways your spouse can meet each need as you define it.

3. Share and communicate with your submissive spouse how you defined your needs and how they can be met. Whatever you do be sure to keep in mind that these are done in mutual Love and Respect for each other and agreement is mandatory in all of this.

Notice that women's top need is affection or love, which aligns with God's command for husbands to meet that need by loving their wives. Notice also that men's top need is sex. Respect, the Biblically commanded need to be met by wives, drops to #5. Every single time I've sat with couples there are numerous issues but the underlying problem ALWAYS for the husband is lack of respect from his wife.

My encouragement to men is two-fold:

• Intentionally move Respect to the top of the list and if you're looking for ways to earn her respect, look at her list. It's always good to strive to be a man who is deserving of that respect;

• Submit to her as a servant-leader and ask her to share her greatest need and how you can meet it. Work through each need until they become habit.

Caution: None of this will come naturally. If it did you'd already be doing these things. Both of you will need to pray and rely on the power of The Holy Spirit to give you the initiative and strength to do this by faith. However, I assure you, if you're willing to commit to and intentionally invest in your spouse and marriage you'll be blessed beyond anything you've ever experienced!

MARRIAGE, FAMILY & PARENTING GOD'S WAY

> *"Marriage and family are both the building
> blocks, and a reflection, of Christ's Church."*

> *"Behold, children are a gift of the LORD, the fruit
> of the womb is a reward. Like arrows in the hand
> of a warrior, so are the children of one's youth."*
>
> (Psalm 127:3-4 NASB)

My prayer and hope with this book is to encourage everyone, but especially those who call Christ Lord, to recognize God's Divine Covenant order from Creation to Christ's return. I pray that you'll be willing, as His disciples, to live it out first in your marriages and families to strengthen His Church and build His Kingdom.

This book is the message The Lord has laid on my heart, and I've been sharing it for over 25 years. It has helped hundreds, if not thousands, to walk in His Divine order, see the blessing in their lives and homes, and be a blessing in His Church and beyond. It begins in the Home.

Dennis Rainey, founder of FamilyLife, one of the best marriage and family organizations in the world today, said this, "Every family is a little church." If we are not doing the job in line with God's Word in our little churches, then it matters little how much we're doing in our "big" churches. If we will follow His design, I truly believe He has much more in store for our lives and He can and will use us to ignite His Church and impact a lost and dying world!

We've heard over and over again that youth are leaving the church and their faith when they go off to college and the stats bear this out although some return later. Ken Ham, founder of The Creation Museum, Answers in Genesis, and The Ark Encounter wrote a book entitled, Already Gone, in which he postulates with some research, that most of our youth are checking out mentally and spiritually in their early teens and middle school years. They simply continue to attend church because parents have the car keys, wallets and final say.

He goes on to say, "'Church today is mostly driven by man-made traditions and not by the biblical mandates to defend the Word of God and live by the Word of God."

***In God's design and mandate, discipleship is to begin
in the home and the church benefits and is stronger when
this happens. When it's not happening, there's not enough
"church" to overcome what is lacking in the home.***

CHAPTER 21

TWO CONTRASTING STORIES OF HOME

Regulars in Church but a Family
Apart from God's Divine Order

I received a call one day from a dad who'd heard me speak at a men's gathering. He asked if we could meet. We worked out a good time and on the appointed day he arrived at my office. As usual I spent a few minutes explaining the foundational principles of Love & Lordship. I told him I would be as gracious as possible but would not shy away from direct questions and comments. I also assured him he could tell me as much or as little as he liked but to please be truthful.

He then told me he was struggling with two teen sons, 18 and 13, and wanted to know how to discipline them without losing their trust or damaging their relationship, as it had been very good up until the last year or so.

I asked what the circumstances were and he shared that he and their mom had been going through a long, drawn out divorce that had lasted several years. They were not living together but he continued to maintain regular and strong contact as they practiced joint custody of the boys.

He talked about how, as the older son had moved further into the teen years his disrespect and even defiance had grown and it was rubbing off on his younger brother. I asked a few questions and gave him some advice about clear communication and boundaries and being sure that he was consistent in his follow-through with both reward and punishment. We closed the session and I told him to let me know if he'd like to meet again.

He called me the next day to set up another meeting and when he arrived it was evident that he was troubled. He said things had gotten worse as he applied the counsel I'd given him. I knew it was solid counsel so I asked him to tell me more about his relationship with his wife and the living arrangements.

What he shared next was a far too common occurrence in our culture and churches today. He said that his relationship with his soon-to-be ex-wife was not good at all. He revealed that, while he had his own place, he was living with another woman who had a young special needs child.

I asked about church and he said they had raised their children in church and continued to attend. That's where he'd met his live-in and her child and things were great with them while things were awful with his wife. He told how wonderful it was to help out with his girlfriend's child, how much good it was doing, and their regular weekly church attendance.

The veil had been removed. Here was a man who had decided to divorce his wife, and though the divorce was not final, live with another woman and justify it because they had met in church, and he was helping her with her special needs child. As we talked further it became clear he was sure God was OK with this arrangement.

I looked him directly in the eye and said, "Sympathy does not change God's Truth or our need for repentance. You told me you came to me because of what I'd shared about integrity. I'm telling you that you are not living with integrity."

I asked him what his boys thought of all of this. He said he really noticed that things had gone from bad to worse when he took on this "new family."

I told him that he could continue the discipline practices we had discussed but "as long as you are not walking in integrity and purity then it is going to be extremely difficult to accomplish the discipline and respect you desire from your boys." He looked puzzled.

I explained that the first thing he needed to do was break away from his live-in and live according to God's Word. I reminded him that his older son was a young man now and likely would continue to pull away unless his dad changed his lifestyle and gave him someone he could look up to. The younger son would probably continue to follow suit.

Finally I said that this distance would likely continue because they were not seeing someone worthy of respect in their father.

If he truly desired to help his sons become the Godly men he said he wanted them to become, then he needed to model it for them. He could put in place all the proper rules and guidelines and hold them accountable, but he would reap what he was sowing and it was clear that he was not sowing good seeds while desiring and expecting good fruit in his sons.

I would like to say that he took my advice and all went well, but I never saw him again. The last I heard things had gone from bad to worse.

A Family Walking in God's Divine Order

"I took my daughter to an Italian restaurant and bought her a promise ring with little diamonds embedded in the band... This outing wasn't completely awkward because my daughters and I were already in the habit of going out on little dates. During my dinner with Jessica, I spent the first portion of our time telling her all the things that I liked about her. As I talked her eyes were welling up with tears...

"I bent down low, leaned in close to her and said Jessica, I am giving you this ring today. Are you willing to make a covenant before the Lord tonight, that on your wedding night you will be prepared to present this ring to your husband and say to him,"This ring represents a covenant I made with my dad that I would save myself for marriage. I have done so."

"Jessica will you wear this ring? As I slipped the ring on her finger I told her that she is no longer a little girl. She is now a woman... As I reflect on my daughter's life since that moment, the growth in her life has been remarkable..."

— Ed Tandy McGlasson, *The Difference A Father Makes*

WOW! What a difference in integrity, humility, purity and the seeds sown by these two fathers.

A child's first concept of God, good or bad, centers on what they see in their earthly parents and particularly the father. The first, and likely most lasting concept, of authority is derived from a child's parents.

That authority, because it is from The Author, must include integrity, purity, humility and character that God has given us in His Word and called us to as parents.

CHAPTER 22

GOD'S DESIGN FOR PARENTING & FAMILY

Since God is our perfect Heavenly Father, we would be wise to seek His counsel for good parenting. He has made it very clear what He expects of us as parents.

1) Parents are the primary disciplers and educators of their children. In Deuteronomy 6:1-9, Moses gathers the leaders of all the tribes, clans and families to share the most important things that God wanted them to know and impress on future generations (vv. 1-3) as they went in to possess the Promised Land. Here are the three things that were of paramount importance (the first two will sound very familiar):

    - God is the One and Only True God—worship only Him (v. 4)

    - Love God with all you are (v. 5)

    - The laws and commands (disciplines) that I will give you—make sure that you teach them to your children—post them and teach them everywhere and at all times (vv. 6-9)

    Parents, we are to take the first and highest responsibility for training our children—not the school, not the government, not coaches, not even pastors or ministers. All these can play a role and help, but what is taught must begin with us and be in line with God's Word and commands!

2) Discipling and educating our children requires time and effort. We find in both the Old and New Testaments what is required of parents.

    Most are familiar with Proverbs 22:6 (NASB): "Train up a child in the way he should go, even when he is old he will not depart from it." This is echoed in Ephesians 6:4 (NASB), again with the fathers as the focal point of this command: "Fathers, do not provoke your children to anger, but bring them up in the discipline and instruction of the Lord."

    There is an ancient proverb, "Bend a tree when it is young." This is an excellent explanation of Proverbs 22:6 for two reasons. First, bending a tree requires ongoing attention and effort just as children do. You can't bend it once and expect it to stay in place. With children, as is strongly implied in the Hebrew text, we as parents must take the time to get to know them, their personalities, strengths and weaknesses, and teach and train them in character consistently over time, being there to help them navigate their struggles and trials. This can't be done with occasional gifts of time, money, or stuff. One of the greatest deceptions from the pits of hell is, "Quality time equals quantity time."

Second, one of the greatest recipes for rebellion is to give the disciplines for developing character and then not being present and/or not walking with integrity in those disciplines yourself. Far too many children have been victims of a parent who comes home only to administer punishment and demand obedience without being present to model behavior. Rules without relationships = rebellion! Train your children to walk in the way they should go by first walking that path yourself.

Monte Wilkinson, Lead Minister at Northeast Christian Church, Lexington, KY, was in our wedding and I consider him a good friend. He shared a wonderful maxim with me when he found out we were expecting our first child: "Children are the greatest blessing and greatest burden all rolled into one." God's Word declares that children are a reward or heritage from The Lord (Psalm 127). If we only see the burden, then we miss the joys of His blessing to us. Scripture also declares that there is a burden in the responsibility of training them up in The Lord (Proverbs 22:6; Ephesians 6:4). If we only looking for blessings, then we miss the lessons and needed pruning in our lives and in our children's as well.

3) Finally, the message from God's Word is that parenting must begin and continue with us in our families and not be abdicated to the church, school, or any other place. Integrity in life, marriage, and parenting makes for authenticity and walking in the True Authority that we have been given in Christ!

Two sad stories drive home this final point.

I was asked to lead a men's retreat a few years ago and was excited to do so as I'd heard many good things about the host church and its men's ministry.

On the Sunday morning when I finished my final teaching, several men came up to share their stories. The two that follow stood out and I believe it was The Holy Spirit that prompted the men to ask me to share them, anonymously of course, to encourage others to take to heart the message of God's Covenant order in Love and Lordship.

Their deepest concern was that they had done exactly as so many others had. They had followed their church's mantra of making the church itself the focal point of their family and faith rather than making the family their focal point. They both mentioned that much lip service had been paid to the home, but it was evident that supporting the church and its ministries and programs was what was expected, even to the detriment of their marriage and family time.

The Church Prioritized

The first father/grandfather was in his mid-70s and retired from a very prominent position in the community. He had been a deacon and an elder at a rapidly growing church and I had known him for years. "Greg, we did exactly what you described in your teaching with regard to making the church the most important thing in our life and family. We spent most of our time going to and from church functions—for their sake."

He went on to say, "We had a good home, but, we spent most of our time doing church without prioritizing Christ." He paused, and with tears flowing freely said, "We did exactly as you described, showing up at every function, making our kids go to every youth group, retreat and event, which they fully enjoyed, but something was clearly missing. Now neither of our children attend church and our grandchildren have never darkened the door of a church."

I shared with him, "I believe you do have a good marriage and home that just got sidetracked as so many have. Continue to show your children and grandchildren the agape love of God in your marriage and with them, and trust they will return and in doing so know more fully what it means to live in His Love and Lordship." He hugged me and thanked me.

The Church Comes First

As I watched the previous gentleman walk away in tears my heart was heavy, but I also realized The Spirit was getting His message through. One man remained.

"I'm in my late 60s. I was married right out of Bible College, trained in preaching, a full-time seminarian, full-time bi-vocational pastor and within a few short years we had two boys. After hearing your message on God's Covenant order, priority of relationships, and relational servant-leadership, I just had to share my story," he said.

He asked me, "What do you think got left out?" I replied, "Your marriage and your wife." He told me that for nearly 20 years he had done what he'd been taught. He had told his wife that she was not strong enough if she couldn't accept him putting the church ahead of her, the marriage, and their family. She eventually had enough, said he was "having an affair with Christ's Bride" and divorced him. It was the most painful thing in his life.

He remarried but the negative impact was strong and remained. He left the ministry and became a successful businessman, keeping a good relationship with his sons.

His sons grew up and went out on their own. His oldest got married, moved away and had a child, the first grandchild. His family was active in the church and that was a comfort.

His younger son got married and moved away as well. He knew this son had not been active in church as an adult. A few years into their marriage they were asked if they could visit during a long weekend. They were excited and anticipated some great news.

They arrived on a Thursday evening and there was a party announcing that they were expecting their first child. He told me it was a wonderful weekend until Saturday night and he decided to ask, "So where are we going to church in the mor...?" His intent was to see if his youngest son and wife were active in church again.

Before he could even finish the final word, his son interrupted and said, "Dad, I don't want to hear a thing about your church or your Jesus. I've seen what His love was like in you and mom and I don't want any part of it."

The man closed, saying, "That's what I wanted you to hear and share. My son saw us attend church every Sunday, me preach most every Sunday and care for many in the church. But the greatest impact was the one that God always intended in our marriage and I had neglected it so I could 'serve Him.' My son saw that and he wanted no part of it. Thank you for your message and keep teaching it."

This is the result of priorities lived out with good intentions but apart from the Truth of God's Word. It has been and is repeated by many who've grown up in the church as pastor and spouse, pastors' kids, church leaders!

If Christ is our priority then His Church will flourish and be blessed through our marriages, families, and relationships reflecting His image and His love for His Bride!

CHAPTER 23

CHARACTER IN SCRIPTURE

Ralph Waldo Emerson wrote, "Happy will that house be in which relations are formed from character." We all desire a home filled with happiness and peace and it is Godly character that makes it a reality. Scripture speaks to the importance of character over and over again. I want to share two passages.

The first is known as "The Prayer of Jabez" in 1 Chronicles 4:9-10 (NASB): "Jabez was more honorable than his brothers, and his mother named him Jabez saying, 'Because I bore him with pain.' Now Jabez called on the God of Israel, saying, 'Oh that You would bless me indeed and enlarge my border, and that Your hand might be with me, and that You would keep me from harm that it may not pain me!' And God granted him what he requested."

We find one simple note about character in the opening and closing statements of these verses. God granted Jabez's request, but the writer of Chronicles did not want us to miss that Jabez was honorable, which means "of noble character," and that is connected to God granting his request.

The second passage points to how character prompts us to act. In Acts 17:11, Paul and Silas had come to Berea from Thessalonica. The text reads, "Now the Berean Jews were of more noble character than those in Thessalonica, for they received the message with great eagerness and examined the Scriptures every day to see if what Paul said was true." Notice what their character prompted them to do. They eagerly searched and studied for themselves. These are key attributes of the discipleship life and what we, as parents, desire to instill in our children.

Character in Parenting – Building Our Children's Self-Worth

Every parent desires to have good children. For those of us who call Christ Lord and walk as His followers and disciples, character is based on His life and God's Word. Everything in this book is founded on God's Word and the principles related here are for building character in our children and ourselves that forms the character of Christ.

One of the enemy's greatest tricks is to reward one another based on accomplishment or performance rather than character. While we need to be encouraged when we have done what is right or good, true development happens in our heart in the formation of character.

As parents we should be attentive to this and dig deeper to find the issues of character so we can praise, reward and help develop that inward compass in our children's lives.

This is a blessing to them as they mature and it is also a tremendous blessing to us as parents to see the self-control and self-discipline develop. This helps create the peaceful home we all desire.

The world is mesmerized by self-esteem but that is just another prideful motive that ultimately destroys. The jewel that our children need is to know their self-worth. Let me give you a simple yet profound equation that I pray will help you in developing this in your children and home:

Self-discipline/self-control ⇨ self-respect ⇨ self-worth ⇨ self-love

This aligns with the greatest commands because it takes self-discipline/control to die to self and worship God above all. As we mature in our faith and praise, we grow to love Him with all that we are. This produces the self-respect that comes from knowing and loving who we are in Him, which gives us our self-worth.

Unless we are willing to practice the self-discipline/control that forms the character in our lives, we will never develop the self-respect and self-worth needed to go outside ourselves and love others fully.

If you would like a great resource that helps identify the character traits of God, I highly recommend Character First, which has done an incredible job identifying God's traits found in Scripture.

This chart can help you be a parent who looks for and praises character as much and more than accomplishment.

Two Kinds of Praise

For **Accomplishment**	For **Character**
• Good grades	• Patience
• Touchdowns	• Responsibility
• Chores	• Initiative
	• Self-Control

Although I didn't apply it immediately, I learned this lesson from my parents on my high school basketball Senior Night. We were ranked #2 in the state and were playing the #10 team.

The score was tied with less than 20 seconds remaining. The other team had the ball and I stole it and went down and scored the winning basket as time expired. The packed gymnasium went nuts and I was carried on people's shoulders, told I was the greatest thing going, and the praise carried over to the dance that followed.

My parents had reminded me that I had to be home 30 minutes after the dance, as always, so we could get up early and be about our farm work. I reluctantly obeyed, as it was hard to pull away from all the praise.

Now, for the powerful lesson. When I came down to breakfast the next morning my Mom and Dad recounted the game and told me that the last shot was awesome and that's what everyone would remember.

But my Mom told me that on their way home they talked very little about the shot and the win. They talked about the hours upon hours upon hours when no one was watching that I'd spent out by the dairy barn shooting baskets and practicing my skills.

That's what they remembered and they wanted me to remember it as well. As I said, it didn't sink in right away, but over time it has become entrenched that my character is what really matters. I thank The Lord for parents who helped me learn that.

Character, Integrity & Legacy

Research shows over and over again that despite the Internet, media, peers and other influencers, parents still have by far the greatest influence on their children. My question to you is, "What legacy will your influence leave?" Will it be one of character that leads them to walking with Christ or will it be for the world?

The second greatest influence is their faith. How are you guiding and helping to shape their faith. It's not the pastor or youth minister's job, it's yours. They will stand or fall based on how you model and instill that faith in them.

Remember, whatever you invest in your children will become the legacy that you leave. You need to be willing to have candid discussions teaching them about life, relationships, and sexuality. Don't let fear, guilt or any other deterrents keep you from being the ones, as parents, to teach your children.

> *"What can you do to promote world peace?*
> *Go home and love your family."*
> — Mother Teresa

CHAPTER 24

BIBLICAL DISCIPLESHIP·
IN PARENTING

Loving Discipline & Punishment

Parenting is ultimately about discipling your children to know Christ as their Savior and Lord and to grow in Him. Discipleship includes teaching, training, Godly discipline, and loving punishment in line with Biblical values, training your children in righteousness according to God's Word.

Biblical Discipline is actually the boundaries, guidelines, and foundations on which you establish or build your marriage, family, parenting (all relationships for that matter): Wisdom, Virtue, Purity, Integrity, Patience, Self-control, and many more all based on the foundation of God's Word—Absolute Truth. Biblical Punishment is actually what occurs when we fail to stay 'inside' or intentionally move 'outside' the disciplines that have been established in order to guide someone back within those truths where they can most fully and freely grow—Deuteronomy 6:4-9; Proverbs 22:6; Ephesians 6:1-4; Hebrews 12:1-15.

Keys to Biblical (& Healthy) Discipline & Punishment

The following is to help you establish disciplines and guidelines and administer loving punishment as needed according to God's Word and our Heavenly Father's example found in Hebrews 12:1-15.

1) Discipline and punishment are both part of God's Truth and Love toward us—His Word must be the source in establishing discipline and administering punishment.

2) Discipline is modeled first in our lives before applied in others—lessons are caught more than taught.

3) Be clear and consistent—both discipline and punishment must be clearly communicated and consistently applied in your life and in parenting.

4) Three guidelines for punishment:
   - Disrespect–ignorant or initial willfulness;
   - Defiance–clear, continued rebellion toward your authority;
   - Danger–to avoid harm and teach lessons that protect from danger.

5) Never punish in anger or from pride–be sure to check your own motives and selfishness whenever applying punishment with your children–very difficult in tense and embarrassing moments, but punishment must be applied in Love.

6) Punishment and reward – Punishment fits the crime; give opportunities to reward for good behavior and heart as well as for good response to punishment (train the heart). Be sure to connect both punishment and reward with character rather than just accomplishment or performance.

7) Involve your children – allow them to help establish foundations and guidelines based on God's Word as you craft and communicate discipline and punishment. Allow them to define their own punishment to the extent they understand the heart issues and can apply it justly. You keep the final say!

God is very straightforward in His Word that His punishment (the literal word in Greek is mastigoó in Hebrews 12:6 is translated as "to scourge" or "to whip") comes to everyone He receives as His child. Why? Because He loves to punish us? Absolutely not, as that makes no sense based on the rest of the story that Christ gave us culminating in The Cross. He then states in verse 8 that if we do not receive the correction, implying punishment, then we are actually not His children.

This is certainly not to advocate child abuse of any kind, but it is to help us understand that punishment is part of God's love and He knows that we will need it as sinful people in a fallen world. I say often, "God is willing to place the 1,000 volt fence before the 1,000 foot cliff. The shock may hurt but you have the chance to learn from it rather than walk off the cliff."

As Ami and I were raising our children our prayer and desire was for them to know all of God's love, knowing that every bit of it, even the tough and sometimes painful part, was for their good. Knowing that as His child, they would at some point receive His punishment out of His love, and instead of them running from it and rebelling against Him we wanted them to see His love and run toward Him.

As they have faced their own consequences and His loving, yet tough, punishment we have seen that prayer come to pass and are so excited about how He has drawn them to Him and grown them in Him!

Three Opportunities for Parents to Disciple/Train Children – Deuteronomy 6:4-9

1) "Family Time"– meals together, devotionals, family worship, other–all of these offer excellent times for stories, family history, recaps of the day, and provide great chances to go deeper in laughter, tears and emotion and especially in teaching and building character and relationships.

2) "Along the Road"–school/team trips, road trips, vacations, drive time appointments, other–more opportunities to focus the conversation through updates on school events, friends, teams, etc., and include character and relationship development.

3) "Milestones"–special times and events, Rites of Passage, Passing on a Blessing, others–Focus on God's design and order, including Jewish culture of Biblical times and young adulthood at 12 (female) and 13 (male) years of age (bat or bar mitzvah) with mature adulthood at 30 years of age (Jesus even honoring this in Public Ministry–Sermon on the Mount)

   - Rites of Passage–Family Crest or Symbol captured and given in some way to children along with family and friends' letters of encouragement and challenge for each child at young adulthood

   - Ongoing discussions at age-appropriate times (beginning by age 3 with respect for body parts, etc.) about bodies, sexuality and relationships

CHAPTER 25

OUR FAMILY STORY: DISCIPLING OUR CHILDREN

Ami and I developed disciplines, guidelines and boundaries in line with God's Word. Any punishments came after talking through with our children the motive or heart issue. They usually came up with a harsher punishment than we would because they had to talk and think through the state of their heart that led to their disobedience or sinful actions.

We as parents could then encourage them to receive the loving punishment without grumbling or complaining (Philippians 2:14-15) and they usually did so. We were then able to show them "grace" by giving back or reducing the punishment before the timeframe they had set—truth (disciplines and punishment) and grace (receiving something back or reducing their punishment).

Another thing that we did that our children have told us was very powerful: We recognized significant moments in their lives (graduations, special awards, moving out on their own, etc.) with special celebrations with just that child which included a letter outlining what we had observed in them on their path to that moment.

The most impactful one for each of them was on their 13th birthday. We developed a ring that included the Williams Family Crest. When I played basketball in Ireland someone researched our family name and presented me with a silver platter with our crest and motto– Williams in Gaelic means "Wisdom in Strength." How awesome...and daunting... is that?

The crest on the ring was the centerpiece and on each side we had engraved a Scripture; on one side was Proverbs 9:10: "The fear of the LORD is the **beginning of wisdom**." On the other side was Philippians 4:13: "I can do all things through Christ **who strengthens me**." "Wisdom in Strength" (emphasis added).

I close this chapter with what will sum up what I've been sharing about Love, Lordship, discipleship, relationships, marriage and family. It repeats a previous story but I pray that you will take it to heart in applying this book's principles in your life and relationships for His Kingdom and Glory.

"Best Decisions I've Made as a Father"

I shared the story about being contacted twice and offered the position of national spokesperson for a rising nonprofit. My decision to turn that position down for the sake of my marriage and family flowed from the priorities that The Lord had revealed in my life.

Here are other decisions that I've made that I hope will encourage you as parents as you strive to train your children up in The Lord:

1) Loving Christ as Lord and pointing my children to their Heavenly Father.

   This is not just claiming His free gift of salvation and showing up at church from time to time or even on a regular basis. This is making Him the first priority and thought in every choice I've made in my life and spending time in His Word and prayer EVERY day for the past 33+ years. He is the Source if we will avail ourselves of Him, and He must be FIRST (Luke 14:25-35) and as He is so prioritized our children have a much greater chance of knowing Him.

2) My children know they are third, and are blessed for it.

   My children know that Christ is first and my wife, their mom, and our marriage is the second highest priority in my life. They have benefited greatly from seeing this lived out, not always perfectly but always striving for it. I know because I've heard them share this openly with their friends when they've seen chaos in other relationships and homes.

3) Saying "No" to other great opportunities.

   Turning down coaching positions with several schools and universities as well as coaching and playing opportunities overseas and at home because it wasn't best for my family.

4) Choosing to schedule all of my life – limiting time away from home.

   I don't just put work or social events on my calendar; I put time with my wife and children on my calendar and mark them as priorities. Very few "emergencies" take priority over them. Recall the previous story about the two opportunities to be a national spokesperson. Each time my decision was prompted by my love (commitment) for my Lord, my wife, and family above all else.

5) Being their mentor, literally their coach and discipler.

Every dad has the opportunity to do this in one or more areas of their children's lives. It doesn't matter to them if you've coached before or are even very good at it. Most of our children will never make a living from sports or entertainment but they will make a life from the things they learn from us. Coaching them is an invaluable opportunity to pass on great life lessons and instill the character of Christ.

6) Choosing to be a man of integrity, modeling what I asked and expected of them.

Every one of us will leave a legacy. We don't get a choice in that. We do get a choice as to what that legacy will be. I've made my share of mistakes but I learned early on that my life needed to match up with what I say. And what I say needs to be in line with God's Word. How you handle and grow from mistakes says as much about who you are to your children as when you get things right.

7) Saying, "I'm sorry, I was wrong, please forgive me."

One of the greatest lessons I've learned is to choose to be humble, confess my errors, and plainly ask for forgiveness. This has been a blessing in my life and has positively impacted my wife and my children. It's made me a better father and allowed me to have a great relationship with each of my children and that is a wealth far greater than earthly riches!

Practicing What We Preach –
Our Children in Their Own Words

Greg Williams. Where to start? Servant and follower of Christ Jesus. Husband to my mother, Ami...and my father. He is a very smart, and very wise man because he lets the Lord lead him in every aspect of his life, and he has set a prime example to my family and to others on how to love the Lord, and others.

The message in this book is the same message that he has taught my siblings and me since we were able to understand, and that is that we are to accept Christ as not only our Savior, but also as our Lord. He has done this in so many ways, through his fatherhood, his servant leadership to my mother and also to us as his children. He's taught me and my brother what it means to be a Godly man, and why that looks so different from the concept of manhood we have in our society today.

He has shown us what it means to love God first, and that without this we cannot truly understand how to love others. Love and Lordship is such an integral part of not only what my dad teaches, but also who he is as a follower of Christ, a husband, and a father.

My dad's teaching has touched my life in so many ways, and has made me the man that I am today, and I truly believe that it will touch your life as well. My dad always says, not my will, but God's will be done, and that is the attitude that I try to take into every aspect of my life, and I hope that by the end of this book, you'll do the same.

— Lansing Williams

If you know anything about my dad, you know he practices what he preaches. I am 24 years old, and in my entire life all my memories of my parents have been unwaveringly consistent with God's Word. This has been true in their marriage, their roles as husband and father, wife and mother, and in their parenting.

In their marriage, I have seen my father lead as Christ leads His Bride, the Church. He has exhibited Christ-like faithfulness, firmness, and love to my mom day after day, year after year. As with every relationship, they did not always agree, but my dad was gracious enough to hear my mom out, listen to her wisdom, and come to an agreement with truth and love. My mother has been a constant companion to my dad, lovingly and willfully submitting to his leadership and servanthood. She was always comfortable voicing her opinion when she disagreed, and knew she was heard and loved unconditionally. She reciprocated that love every day, without fail. Despite the hard times, whether financially, spiritually, or relationally, they have stood by one another as best friends and godly lovers. As a son, I always knew I had amazing examples of parents and a godly marriage.

In their parenting, my mom and dad were partners. They were a team, working together to raise my siblings and me to the best of their ability and trusting God to fill in the gaps where they fall short. When we messed up, they always gave us "punishment that fit the crime," and always out of love and truth. As I've grown into a young man, I wouldn't trade anything to have any other parents in my life. I was always sure that my parents loved me and wanted what was best for me, an excellent example of God's love to His children.

My parents are by no means perfect. They made mistakes, as every human being does. However, I had a daily example of what it means to be a good husband, father, and godly man in my dad. I knew what kind of wife and mother I wanted to love because I had an amazing example in my mom. They have faithfully lived out love and lordship in their 29 years of marriage, and I know they will continue to do so until death do they part.

— Harrison Williams

Something that I've always admired about my dad was his ability to selflessly love my mom. This trait has been important to me for a long time, because as I've grown up and been able to see myself become more and more like my mom, it's characteristics like these that I know I can't compromise on when it comes to finding my husband. Ever since I was old enough to understand, and now being almost 21 years old, I've seen several qualities within my parents' marriage that I knew I needed to experience within my own, whenever that day comes.

My parents, especially my dad, instilled within me from a young age the importance of godly relationships, from friendships to my future husband and marriage. I know that I am extremely blessed to have had such a wonderful example throughout my life, not only of what I want to see in my future relationship, but also the qualities I need to seek out in a husband, the qualities I will need to uphold as someone's wife, and of course, all the ways I want to be able to parent just like my parents did.

My parents have always strived to live their lives in accordance with God's Word, and I know that my family has been blessed beyond measure because of this. My parents have shown me what marriage truly is. Not only that they are two individuals that have become one, but ultimately how the marriage of one man and one woman is symbolic of Christ and His Bride, the Church.

They've taught me that marriage isn't sunshine and rainbows until death do you part, but that loving the person you've chosen to spend the rest of your life with is not a feeling—it's a daily choice. They've taught me that marriages don't succeed because both parties said "I do" 29 years ago, but instead they say it every day.

I've grown up learning about the biblical context of marriage, but just to learn about it is a very different thing from being able to watch it being lived out every day within your own home. This blessing is something I never want to take for granted, especially when I one day separate from my family and start one of my own. I truly admire my parents' love for each other and their love for my brothers and me, and while it isn't perfect by a long shot, I know that I have seen and will continue to see it be blessed as they continue their walks with Christ individually and within their relationship to each other.

This book has been a long time coming. I remember my dad praying every night about starting this project when I was 14 or 15 years old, and as his daughter, I can honestly say that I am extremely proud to watch him pursue his passion and be blessed throughout the journey.

— Haidyn Williams

I pray for those who are parents that you are encouraged to be the father and mother that He has placed you in your family to be. Ultimately I pray your children know their Heavenly Father through Christ as their Savior and Lord because of what they've seen in you.

Know this...it's never too late to begin making the decisions and living the life that point your family and children to Him!

"I have disposed of all my property to my family. There is one thing more I wish I could give to them, and that is the Christian religion. If they had that and I had not given them one cent, they would be rich. If they have not that, and I had given them the world, they would be poor."

— Patrick Henry

STUDY GUIDE
MARRIAGE, FAMILY & PARENTING GOD'S WAY

Key Concepts

1) In God's design, every family starts with marriage: one man/one woman for life.

2) Families are the "building blocks" of Christ's Family, The Church.

3) Developing Godly character or the heart of Christ should be the first priority in parenting—discipling them in the nurture and admonition of the Lord!

4) Children are a gift from The Lord, the greatest blessing/burden rolled into one.

5) Parenting is the first and most powerful depiction of Godly Love and Authority in a child's life and is to reflect God's image in His Truth and Love.

6) Parenting is to reflect the Love and Authority of God according to His Truth revealed in His Son, His Word and His Spirit.

7) Parenting moves children from respect for parental authority to self-control and respect for God's Authority in Christ.

8) Parenting includes loving discipline and punishment, ultimately discipling our children in Christ.

9) Discipline includes the foundations, guidelines and boundaries, in line with God's Word and Truth, in which we can most fully and freely mature and grow.

10) Punishment is the loving, corrective response to our children when they step outside the established disciplines in line with God's Word.

11) Punishment should never be done in anger or from pride but in love and humility to disciple our child's heart rather than simply change behavior.

12) Three D's to consider when administering loving punishment:
    • Disrespect • Defiance • Danger.

Key Questions

1) What is God's design for marriage, family, and Christ's Church?

2) What is the first priority for parents with their children?

3) What is the role of parents in discipline, loving punishment, and discipleship?

4) What are the 3 D's that indicate a need for loving punishment?

Discussion

1) How can you train for character rather than just behavior change?

2) Discuss the Biblical connections among love, authority, discipleship, discipline, and punishment.

3) What does the Character of Christ look like in us as we parent our children?

4) How are you praising and encouraging—loving— your children? What legacy is it leading to?

THE HOME & RELATIONAL SERVANT- LEADERSHIP IN CHRIST'S FAMILY

> *"Strength of character may be acquired at work, but beauty of character is learned at home. There the affections are trained. There the gentle life reaches us, the true heaven life. In one word, the family circle is the supreme conductor of Christianity."*
>
> — Henry Drummond

"It is a trustworthy statement: if any man aspires to the office of elder (or overseer), it is a fine work he desires **to do... He must be** one who manages his own household well, keeping his children under control with all dignity (but if a man does not know how to manage his own household, how will he take care of the church of God?)." (1 Timothy 3:1, 4-5) (NASB, emphasis in original text)

In God's Covenant design, how are we to build the loving fellowship of believers as His Church except that we first, just as He did, begin with the loving relationships of marriage and family? This is where both love and leadership are trained and matured in God's design and according to His Word. When we miss it here the church is crippled. Today's church is crippled!

CHAPTER 26

OUR FAMILIES
& CHRIST'S FAMILY

As I begin this section, I think it's imperative that we make the connection between the Bible's picture of the nuclear and extended family as God created them to be and His Family, known as Christ's Church. These are inseparable in God's Covenant order and design.

Andrew Walker wrote a great article entitled "The Church as Forged Family: A Response to David Brooks" at Institute for Family Studies in early 2020. In his response to Brooks' "The Nuclear Family Was a Mistake" in The Atlantic, Walker states:

"What I want to suggest, however, is that Brooks' call for the "forged family" can already be found in an institution so familiar to us that its routineness makes us blind to its offerings. I am speaking of the local church—not the abstract, universalized "the church." The church remains a pillar of American civil society, and while it has traditionally played an irreplaceable role in forging community, as church participation has declined and the spiritually fluid increase, people are now able to seek forged families elsewhere. And while those who seek it elsewhere may find it, there is no other institution more apt to be the central force in forging family and social connections than the local church."

My point here is to help forge the tie between God's design for the nuclear and extended relationships that make up our families and the family that is the Church of Christ. Below are a number of Scriptures that refer to the Church as a family or household, reinforcing Walker's point about God's role for relationships in family—yours, mine and His.

Galatians 6:10 (household of the faith); Ephesians 2:19-22 (God's household); 1 Timothy 3:5 (household or family, church), 1 Timothy 3:15 (household of God); 1 Peter 4:17 (household of God) and all point to God's design and purpose in creating us in His image, lived out in loving relationships in our families and in His family, Christ's Church.

This is why I believe the enemy battles so fervently to bring down our marriages and families. I also believe it is why he laughs when we do not prioritize our marriages and homes in helping to build Godly relationships. Home is where we learn to love, lead and disciple, and the Church benefits from focusing on and helping husbands and wives, mothers and fathers, to do so. Not just attend church and youth group and related activities.

Two Stories of Modern-day Home & Church Leadership

Much of the modern-day Western church has opted for a corporate success model based on marketing principles and attraction rather than a Kingdom fruit model based on disciples maturing and making new disciples as branches in The Vine. (John 15:1-8)

The currency of Christ's Kingdom is loving relationships and the fruit is disciples making disciples, not just in numbers but in obedience and accountability to His Word and Spirit. This is the only way we learn to love and lead according to God's Word.

A Leader in Business & Church...but not at Home

A dear friend and supporter of my ministry came up to me after a men's speaking engagement over 15 years ago. He was a very successful businessman and a long-time elder in a large and influential church.

He began by saying, "Don't do what I've done. Be sure you keep your priorities in the right place as you've shared with us."

He told how at Christmas one year his wife asked how many Sundays he'd been home that year?

"I don't know, 25 or so," he said, assuming Sundays meant "weekends," giving himself more credit than deserved.

She immediately said, "I'm talking about just Sundays as you weren't home one single full weekend."

He replied curtly, "Yes, I was."

She retorted, "How many Sundays this entire year?" Now he was angry and said, "At least half."

She said, "Do you really want to know how many Sundays you've been home with your family this last year?"

"Sure," he quipped.

"You've been home three Sundays the entire year and not one single full weekend or Saturday."

When he denied it she got the calendar and showed him the proof. She then said, "Your daughter is 11 and you've missed her growing up. Your son is now 3. Are you going to miss him growing up as well?"

He told me this got his attention and he began to change his schedule to reflect the change in his priorities, and more importantly, in his heart. I've seen him over the years and he admittedly still struggles, as pride and workaholism continue to challenge him.

He is a wonderful man, and although he was influential in the community, he was not qualified to be an elder in Christ's Church at that time.

Remember Dennis Rainey's quote, "Every family is a little church." In line with God's Word and order, if we are not paying attention to our little churches (marriages and families), then it matters little how big our big churches get. In other words, it doesn't really matter the size or supposed influence of our "big" churches if we are not building strong marriages and families.

God is faithful to use our attempts to build great followings by teaching a "small gospel." But if we will follow His design, I truly believe that He has so much more in store for our lives and He can and will use us to ignite His Church to impact a lost and dying world.

"Having an Affair with Christ's Bride"

I was speaking at a marriage and family conference in Arizona and noticed that one of the other speakers was in my session. I decided to return the favor and join his and heard him tell his story.

He was 10 years out of Bible college and, as he put it, "part of the Biblical Big Three" that was building a fast-growing church in the upper Midwest. "There's the charismatic senior pastor, the dynamic worship leader, and the great youth minister—and I was the great youth minister!" He had been married right out of school, now with two beautiful daughters.

One Friday afternoon he was in his office preparing for another awesome weekend of youth events when his phone rang. He could see that it was his wife so he answered, "Hey honey, what's up?"

"We need to talk," she said.

"Is everyone OK? Are the girls OK?" he asked.

"They're fine," she said. "This is about us. You need to decide, either the ministry or our marriage?"

"What are you talking about," he retorted. "We're, I'm, serving The Lord. We're building this growing church and the youth group is growing like crazy."

"It's either the marriage or the ministry," she said. Click.

He knew she was serious so he called the senior minister. "My wife just gave me an ultimatum: marriage or ministry?"

The senior minister said, "We've been trying to tell you this for eight years."

(To which I thought, "Shame on you, senior minister, you were in a position to be sure that he spent more time at home rather than continue to 'build the church' to the detriment of his marriage and family.")

The senior minister wisely told him to get to his quiet place with The Lord, pray, and get this worked out. There would be no youth activities this weekend. They both would call his wife and confirm the plan.

He called and then got in his car and spent the next 10 minutes driving to his quiet place while "praying"—he actually said he was defending his work for The Lord—questioning why this was happening. When he arrived he spent five more minutes "praying," and then there was a clear interruption in his thoughts. It wasn't audible, but he knew it was The Lord.

"Son, why are you having an affair with My Bride? I can use you to help with her if you will take care of your bride first."

He said it hit him like a ton of bricks and he knew it was The Holy Spirit and, of course, in line with God's Word.

He hurried home to his wife to apologize and ask for her forgiveness. She was skeptical as she'd heard similar things before, but this was different so she accepted his apology and forgave him.

Together they moved out of church ministry and began ministering to marriages and families. In recent years they have helped plant churches based on discipleship in marriage and family ministry.

CHAPTER 27

LOVING & LEADING IN THE HOME & IN HIS CHURCH

I could go on and on with stories of misplaced priorities in our churches where there was very little, if any, discipleship, love, and leadership in line with God's Word. The culture and our churches are evidence we are failing to train and select leaders from our homes; rather, we are choosing those who are successful in the culture and we are being led exactly where such leaders will lead.

> *"The church in America*
> *has become so culturally relevant that*
> *it has become culturally irrelevant."*

The modern American church has become so concerned about reaching the culture to the point that we look much like the culture. While Christ certainly was in the culture, He was careful not to compromise His message or His lifestyle to accommodate those in it:

He prayed, "but now I come to You; and these things I speak in the world so that they may have My joy made full in themselves. I have given them Your word; **and the world has hated them, because they are not of the world, even as I am not of the world.** I do not ask You to take them out of the world, but to keep them from the evil one. They are not of the world, even as I am not of the world. Sanctify them in the truth; Your word is truth. As You sent Me into the world, I also have sent them into the world. For their sakes I sanctify Myself, that they themselves also may be sanctified in truth. 'I do not ask on behalf of these alone, but for those also who believe in Me through their word; that they may all be one; even as You, Father, are in Me and I in You, that they also may be in Us, so that the world may believe that You sent Me.'" (John 17:13-21 NASB) (emphasis added)

We want so badly for His message to be well received that we do so much to get the culture to like and accept it. The intent is good but the results are bad.

God forgive us as we repent and seek His face to follow His commands for leading His Church. Paul wrote a letter to Timothy to take to the churches he had planted that is just as relevant and applicable today if we will heed the Word of The Holy Spirit.

"It is a trustworthy statement: if any man aspires to the office of overseer, it is a fine work he desires to do. An overseer, then, must be above reproach, the husband of one wife, temperate, prudent, respectable, hospitable, able to teach, not addicted to wine or pugnacious, but gentle, peaceable, free from the love of money. **He must be one who manages his own household well, keeping his children under control with all dignity (but if a man does not know how to manage his own household, how will he take care of the church of God?),** and not a new convert, so that he will not become conceited and fall into the condemnation incurred by the devil. And he must have a good reputation with those outside the church, so that he will not fall into reproach and the snare of the devil." (1 Timothy 3:1-7 NASB) (emphasis added)

The word overseer (episkopos in Greek) equates to guardian or shepherd. In Paul's letter to Titus (1:5) the word used translates as elder, pointing to the same thing, denoting a high position of leadership in the church. He continues with similar qualifications for servant-leaders called deacons.

There are seven general qualifications outlined in these verses centered focused on mature faith, personal character and Godly relationships, in particular marriage and family:

1) Must be the husband of one wife (v. 2). For most of church history this meant no polygamy or divorce. Polygamy is still strongly rejected but many churches have chosen leaders who have been divorced and remarried. While subject to interpretation, when we look at the strong teachings regarding marriage, family and relational servant-leadership in God's Word, I think the church for the most part throughout history interpreted it correctly and excluded those who have been divorced from elder and deacon roles. This does not preclude divorcees from other service in His Church with all servant-leading rooted in humility and love above all else.

142

2) He should necessarily be an older person as the Greek word for elder, presbyteros, (Titus 1:5) literally means an older person or advanced in years or life (v. 2—overseer or bishop). With first century life expectancies shorter than ours today, we should apply the principle to a stage of life rather than a specific age based on the other requirements, in particular that of maturity in the faith and servant-leading our families.

3) Ability to teach and lead or shepherd—ability to teach is specifically mentioned and scholars agree that a key role and definition of an overseer or elder is shepherding (v. 2).

4) Personal maturity and behavior—must be mature and disciplined, above reproach, in his behavior personally, relationally, financially and spiritually (vv. 2-3).

5) Mature in the faith—strong in his faith and not a young believer so he is not prone to pride and easily lured away by the flesh and the world (v. 6).

6) Must have a good testimony in the community—reputation here is not by façade or hypocrisy but must be clear evidence of a life well lived (v. 7).

7) Must be able to relationally servant-lead his family—he must be one who lovingly and consistently serves and leads his marriage, wife and children in line with Scriptural teachings on authority. If he can't serve and lead his family then how can he lead Christ's family? (vv. 4-5).

Far too often, leaders are selected on qualifications two through six but only lip service is given to marriage and relational servant-leadership in the home. This has been confirmed over and over again by pastors, elders, and deacons—not to mention their wives—as I have spoken on this topic.

Here's my personal experience to make the point.

I was 39 and a deacon at a large, influential church when three staff members approached me to ask if I would consider nomination as an elder for the upcoming year. My response was very simply, "I'm not qualified."

They looked at me, puzzled, and began to graciously express that they'd heard me teach, had seen evidence in my life and in the lives of others, and knew I had a good testimony in the community. I replied,

"Thanks for your encouraging and humbling words, but you left out one thing. I have three small children at home and I'm called to servant-lead them with my wife and train them up in The Lord."

With puzzled looks they wondered aloud why I would balk because they always saw our family in church. I shared what The Lord had laid on my heart and what I teach on the qualifications listed above and the cultural context in which they were written.

The New Testament, as we know it was predominantly written in and for a Jewish culture and that informs us as to what was being taught. In that culture a boy was treated as a boy until age 13 when he was considered a young man. Girls were considered girls until they were considered a young woman at age 12.

I said to the staff members that I needed to be with my wife and children helping to train them up according to Scripture, at least until those rites of passage. Then I, and others, could evaluate whether I'd servant-led my family according to God's Word and based on the fruit in their lives and our family. I needed to be home rather than away several additional nights each month.

One of the lead pastors asked me if I would come and teach this to the current elders in the church. I said, "Let me know." I'm still waiting.

The very next year I had three elders approach me and ask if they could nominate me for the position of elder. I gave the same answer. They raised the same questions and I gave the same response. I heard little from two of them after that.

I can tell you that it is prominent in our churches that the one qualification that is, shall we say, watered down or ignored is the one that The Holy Spirit prompted Paul to ask: "If a man does not know how to manage or relationally servant-lead, according to God's Word on authority and leadership, in his own family then how can he manage Christ's Family or Church?"

This means we must invest the time, effort, and teaching to train our children to become the Godly young men and women that He desires them to be and entrusted us to make it happen.

CHAPTER 28

THE MARRIAGE ⇨ FAMILY ⇨ CHURCH LEADERSHIP CONNECTION

When we do not elevate the relationships of marriage and family as God's Word prescribes, we fail to put in place the very relationships and related lessons needed to teach love, humility, and relational servant-leadership—all required to build Christ's Church on the apostle's teachings and on Him as the Cornerstone. (Ephesians 2:19-22)

Based on my studies and the context of Scripture regarding the qualifications to build Christ's Church, there are several teachings we should take to heart to develop the loving relationships and relational servant-leadership in our homes and then in His Family, The Church:

1) Understanding of and obedience to Christ's model of leadership as the submissive, humble servant's heart that leads to an invitation of influence—this is True Authority that doesn't change from the family to the Church to the workplace or culture.

2) Relational servant-leadership is learned through the most important and intimate of relationships, that of marriage and family, as we've learned throughout this book.

3) God's Word places a priority on managing (serving) those in the family/home, with no emphasis on cultural or business acumen or savvy.

4) Marriage/Family management or relational servant-leadership must be a priority in choosing servant-leaders in Christ's Church.

Deception & Its Fruit

We must be honest with ourselves and with others if we are going to apply God's Word to our lives, homes, and to Christ's Church. Otherwise we will continue to prioritize cultural success above Kingdom fruit!

In The Screwtape Letters C.S. Lewis has veteran tempter Screwtape reveal a little secret about human beings: we are incurably idealistic. "Do what you will," he warns, "there is going to be some benevolence, as well as some malice, in your patient's soul. The great thing is to direct the malice to his immediate neighbours whom he meets every day and thrust his benevolence out to the remote circumference, to people he does not know. The malice thus becomes wholly real and the benevolence largely imaginary."

We have mastered the art of loving and leading "from afar" in community and systems, such as corporate or governing relationships (including the church), all the while neglecting to be obedient to God's Word to love and lead first in the most intimate of relationships—marriage and family!

Here are several issues to consider as we determine whether and where we are compromising on God's Word and in His Church:

1) PRIDE—It looks a lot better to be on a church board than to do the humble work of raising and training our children as a prerequisite to leading His Church. We must humble ourselves and seek His Word and will above positions of influence or recognition. This is always subtle but prevalent when held up against the standard and teaching that marriage and family must be the precursor to relational servant-leadership in His Church.

2) There is a lack of truth teaching on relationships, sexuality, marriage, and family and relational servant-leadership when it comes to God's command to practice and master it first in the home. As a result of this failure we see the fallout in relationships and leadership in our churches.

3) Marriage/Family is devalued by culture and not truthfully defended by our churches as defined in Scripture...just as long as we're still attending church. We must boldly, firmly, and graciously teach and uphold God's standard for relationships and sexuality, calling out cohabitation, promiscuity, adultery, divorce, homosexuality, polygamy, and pedophilia, all porneia (sexual immorality) for the sins that they are. We must also gently point to freedom and forgiveness found only in Christ.

4) Church leadership decisions conform to the world—because we have elevated building, attendance, and giving to support our assets and programs over discipleship, we prioritize

the corporate, financial business model over relationships and family servant-leadership. We must return to the priorities found in God's Word and trust Him to guide us in loving relationships over budgets and buildings. The Disciple-Making Movements (DMM) and Church Planting Movements (CPM) are finding this the key to making disciples and building His Church apart from property and programs.

5) Experience and humility gained from servant-leading in the family are lost to both the home and the church. When we shortcut God's design and order for discipleship training in relationships in families, then both our families and our churches lose.

Are you serving your marriage, spouse, and family with as much or more time and effort as you are serving those in the church or those the church calls you to serve? It is amazing how often this question stops people in their tracks.

> *"The main characteristic of young modern life today is an intense craving to be interested. Literature, amusements, all indicate this tendency, and in religion the Church is apt to pander to the demand to be interested; consequently men won't face the rugged facts of the Gospel because when the Holy Spirit comes in He challenges a man's will, demands a reconstruction of his whole life, and produces a change of mind which will work havoc in his former complacency."*
>
> — Oswald Chambers, *My Utmost for Highest*

Where are we in the church today as we pander to attract folks without calling them to be Christ's disciple and to call and help others do the same, to die to self so we can truly live for Him?

I ask these questions with nearly every man and couple, and at every event to spotlight God's teaching on true love and relational servant-leadership according to His design and commands:

1) Do you desire to lead in God's Kingdom? Many answer, "Yes."

2) From where will He draw and designate His Kingdom leaders? A few answer, "From His Church."

3) From where does His Word say the leaders in His Church are

to come? Very few offer, "The marriage and family, the home?" (Often questioned rather than answered).

4) Are you preparing yourself to be a leader in His Church, according to His Word, in your marriage and family? Few answer at all.

We must take care to identify and select relational servant-leaders in Christ's Church. They will only be able to take us as far as they've gone. Too many today have gone far in leading the world but not their family. In 1 Timothy 3:4-5, The Holy Spirit, through Paul, poses the poignant question, "How can you lead Christ's family if you can't or aren't servant-leading yours?"

Remember from earlier chapters that Christ is The Author and true authority comes from Him. Relational servant-leadership is His concept and model of authority. We have far too often opted for the culture's pseudo-leadership and brought it into our churches. We must change so we are training leaders in our homes and then in His Church who will truly impact the world for His Kingdom and Glory!

Scriptural and Practical Solutions

How are we to do this? I propose the answers lie in Scripture for training disciples, building Christ-like character and healthy relationships that honor marriage and family, and reflect His Truth and loving image.

As families and The Church focus on these in obedience-based discipleship, we will see the following become much more prevalent in our lives, homes, relationships and in His Body.

Here are seven Scriptural and practical solutions that take us right back through the principles of His Love and Lordship in this book:

1) Christ as Lord is our first priority—we need to seek to know and live in the Love and Lordship of Christ and His model of relational servant-leadership as Authority (Truth). (Matthew 20:24-28; John 13:1-17)

2) Discipleship is our response to His Lordship and how we mature in Him—Ephesians 4:13; Hebrews 5:14; James 1:2-4. We will teach disciples how to first understand God's love for us, followed by loving Him with all we are and then loving who we are in Christ so we can love all others—Matthew 22:37-39; Mark 12:29-31. In doing so we will bear fruit and grow in the knowledge of God. (Colossians 9:1-11; Galatians 5:22-24)

3) Obedience-based discipleship and maturity in Christ will be the priority and evident in Church teaching and in our relationships and service, beginning in the home and family. We do this by prioritizing our relationships in His Covenant Order: Christ⇨Marriage/Family⇨Church⇨World. (Genesis 2:24; Matthew 5:19; Hebrews 13:4; Proverbs 22:6; Ephesians 6:1-4)

4) We mature in discipleship and mentoring and in relationship with Him and others through studying and serving according to His Word–2 Timothy 2:15; Matthew 28:18-20; Hebrews 5:11–6:6. We revalue and rebuild a Kingdom marriage and family culture that emphasizes:
   - Teaching and accountability regarding agape relationships and purity in sexuality;
   - Relational servant-leadership modeled and taught in the home;
   - Generational discipleship beginning in the home and reinforced in churches.

5) This maturation in Christ builds a relational or family-based body of believers rather than corporate and business-based– Ephesians 2:11-22; Ephesians 4. Building relationships is taught as part of Spiritual Disciplines:
   - Discipling/Mentoring, Serving/Servant-leadership flows from applying Scriptures with the understanding that good relationships are formed in the discipline of The Holy Spirit and in line with God's Word rather than just according to our natural, selfish flesh, desires and feelings.

6) We are called to His Covenant priorities and throughout His Word these are familial and relational, rooted in character above performance, growth, financial, and numbers served; business acumen and ability are needed but not prioritized over family and relationships in selecting leaders and in decision-making–1 Timothy 3:1-13; Titus 1:6-10. Our maturity in Christ focuses on and builds a family-based Body or Church rather than a corporate, business-based model driven by outcomes.
   - In following through His Covenant order, we can and will build an Acts 2 familial Church that makes

and grows disciples who serve, give, and share as a result of His priority principles rather than service opportunities and programs masquerading as discipleship leading to shallow faith and lives–Acts 2; Matthew 7:21-23. The Biblical emphasis of discipleship and loving relationships as Kingdom fruit takes priority and drives decision-making with regard to growth, finances, service, programs and all other elements rather than the reverse.

7) A familial and relational Church develops disciples who serve, give, share, and lead as a result of priority principles of Christ's Lordship and our discipleship rather than service opportunities and programs masquerading as discipleship. Service should flow from study and maturity, personally and relationally, and the expectation of, and growth in, obedience rather than preceding it.

CHAPTER 29

"WHAT WOULD JESUS SAY TO TODAY'S MEGACHURCH?"

I was asked to speak at a luncheon for business and church leaders a few years ago and I shared a version of Love & Lordship. Afterward, I noticed one gentleman, an executive minister at a fairly large church, waiting off to the side. He introduced himself and began, "I can't refute a single thing you're saying according to God's Word, but what do you think Jesus would say to today's megachurches?"

I asked if his question implied that Jesus would have a different truth for larger churches.

He said, "I don't think that's what I'm saying, but I'm not really sure." The Lord gave me a very clear answer for his question directly from His Word and from the life of Christ.

"I did speak to several megachurches and my answer is in John 6." It was here that Jesus addressed likely the largest crowd He faced except perhaps for His trial and crucifixion.

Jesus clearly stated that the masses followed Him not because of the signs and miracles He performed but because He fed them and they were hoping for more (v. 26).

He then proclaimed a Truth that was very difficult to swallow, declaring that He was the Bread of Life and that if they did not believe in Him they would not have eternal life. They understood He was saying that the only way for them to have real life was to fully partake of this Bread (the Greek here implies that they would need to voraciously partake of this Bread or they would have no life in them). In other words, they must believe in Him with all their heart or there was no eternal life for them (vv. 51, 53). When He finished many disciples knew it was a very difficult thing He was asking so they walked away (v. 66).

I asked the minister if he thought that was a fair answer to his question and even more importantly was it a Biblical response? He nodded in agreement and, with head bowed and shoulders slumped, walked away.

The Whole Truth

"If a church offers no truth that is not available in the general culture...there is not much reason to pay it attention."

— Richard John Neuhaus

I wholeheartedly believe that most pastors, small or large church, desire for people to know Jesus as Savior and Lord. I also believe that many have gotten caught up in attracting folks rather than truly making disciples. I pray that we take to heart Jesus' words: to place Him above all else; that loving Him is obeying Him; and we begin to prioritize our marriages, families, and homes to obedience-based discipleship in loving relationships that builds His Church and advances His Kingdom. The gates of Hell will not prevail against it!

In the early part of this century the Willow Creek Community Church (WCCC) in the Chicago area was one of the fastest growing and largest churches in America when it launched a discipleship survey to "gauge the depth" of discipleship in their growth.

Before the results were published, WCCC asked 30 of their own church plants across the country to take the survey. Statistically the results were the same as at WCCC. Here's my summary of what they found:

1) There were four groups of people in their church with the largest being "seekers" and "new/young believers." The other two groups were those "maturing in Christ" and "mature in Christ."

2) There was very little movement except growth continued in the first two groups by numbers but not in maturity of their faith.

3) The "mature in Christ" group was disgruntled with church because they weren't being fed.

Needless to say the ministers and staff were shocked. They had thought that for sure their church, being the pioneer of small groups and "discipleship," would have seen tremendous maturation along with the exponential growth in their numbers. The reveal was that while their numbers were exploding, discipleship was not happening, at least not with any significance.

Knowing all this, in 2007 I asked an elder at the church I was attending if anyone had heard of the Reveal survey but he had not and that was the end of the discussion until mid-2008 when this same elder approached me and excitedly said, "Did you hear? We've been selected to do the Reveal survey." I congratulated him and shared one thought: "I don't think we'll ever see or make public the results of that survey in this church or community."

"Really, why?" he asked.

"I don't know that our results will be any different," I said.

The survey was administered in early 2009 to any and all members and regular attendees, many of whom evidently participated with great enthusiasm. The results were to be announced at the end of March.

I approached the elder in mid-April, when the results still hadn't been released, and he shared that they were hoping to have it out in May. In mid-May I was told they were pushing it off until June.

Finally, in mid-June he told me they had decided not to release the findings. Then he looked at me and said, "You told me over a year ago that these findings would never be released. How did you know?"

"I had studied the results and knew that every church that had taken it to this point (all 100+ megachurches) had the same statistical findings. Those findings were that disciples were not being made despite the tremendous growth in buildings, programs, and numbers. I was nearly certain that our church would have the same results and likely would not make those dismal results public."

"That's really sad," he said, and walked away.

How are we really doing when it comes to making disciples, and building loving relationships in our marriages and homes that can stand the test of time and help build the fellowship of believers that is Christ's Church?

This is Christ's command and He has given us all we need to be His disciples and make disciples as we trust in Him and are obedient to His Word.

Only then are we really taking His message to a world that needs it. They will probably not like it initially; but those who have eyes to see and ears to hear the difference cannot help but answer clearly that they desire to be His or want no part of Him. Let's make His Love and Lordship clear so they can know.

"I've often wondered what Jesus' Sermon on the Mount would have looked like if He would have had to run it through most modern-day church boards."

— Ronald Reagan

STUDY GUIDE
THE HOME & RELATIONAL
SERVANT-LEADERSHIP
IN CHRIST'S FAMILY

Key Concepts

1) In God's design, marriage and family is a precursor of loving relationships and
servant-leadership to the family of Christ, The Church.

2) Servant-leadership in The Church is to be practiced and matured in the most intimate of relationships...marriage and family.

3) Elder in Scripture literally means an "older person" strongly inferring wisdom from experience coming from family and other relationships.

4) Spiritual maturity in faith is a requirement for the position of elder in The Church.

5) Teaching and shepherding are two traits to be evident in any potential elder's life.

6) Elders and deacons must exercise Godly character in their home and in the community.

7) Authority in the Home and Church are to reflect Christ's model of servant- leadership.

8) The priority for Church leadership is familial and relational rather than commercial and corporate.

9) Leadership always carries with it the temptation of pride especially when practiced according to the culture rather than God's Word.

10) The Church must step up in supporting marriage and family and in holding members accountable to spiritual and relational health and sexual purity.

11) Humility, experience, and wisdom are gained from marriage and training up children in The Lord. This is essential in servant-leading in Christ's Church.

Key Questions

1) What has been your experience with leadership in your church(es)?

2) Where have you seen good models of servant-leadership in families?

3) Where have you seen good models of servant-leadership in The Church?

4) What do you need to do to lead in your home and/or in His Church according to His Word?

5) How would relational servant-leadership change the way your church's leadership might be structured?

Discussion

1) What is God calling you to do in your family to love and lead more like Christ?

2) Are you preparing yourself in your home to be a servant-leader in Christ's Church?

3) What is the relationship among love, lordship, and servant-leadership?

4) What are you modeling for your children when it comes to love and leading?

SECTION 8

WISE
AS SERPENTS,
GENTLE
AS DOVES

"This is a day when practical work is overemphasized, and the saints who are bringing every project into captivity are criticized and told that they are not in earnest for God or for souls. True earnestness is found in obeying God, not in the inclination to serve Him that is born of undisciplined human nature. It is inconceivable, but true nevertheless, that saints are not bringing every project into captivity, but are doing work for God at the instigation of their own human nature, which has not been spiritualized by determined discipline.

We are apt to forget that a man is not only committed to Jesus Christ for salvation; he is committed to Jesus Christ's view of God, of the world, of sin and of the devil, and this will mean that he must recognize the responsibility of being transformed by the renewing of his mind." *(Emphasis added)*

— Oswald Chambers, *My Utmost for Highest*

"'The body is not only biological. The body, as John Paul II unfolds in great detail, is also theological. It tells an astounding divine story. And it does so precisely through the mystery of sexual difference and the call of the two to become 'one flesh.' This means that sex is not just about sex. The way we understand and express our sexuality points to our deepest-held convictions about who we are, who God is, the meaning of love, the ordering of society, and, ultimately, the mystery of the universe. Hence, John Paul II's Theology of the Body is much more than a reflection on sex and married love. Through that, it leads us to 'the rediscovery of the meaning of the whole of existence…the meaning of life.'

"Christ teaches that the meaning of life is found by loving as he loves (see John 15:12). One of John Paul II's main insights is that God inscribed this vocation to love as he loves right in our bodies by creating us male and female and calling us to become 'one flesh' (see Genesis 2:24). Far from being a footnote in the Christian life, the way we understand the body and the sexual relationships 'concerns the whole Bible.' It plunges us into 'the perspective of the whole gospel, or the whole teaching even more, of the whole mission of Christ.'

"Christ's mission is to restore the order of love in a world seriously distorted by sin. And the union of the sexes, as always, lies at the basis of the human 'order of love.' Therefore, what we learn in

John Paul II's TOB is obviously 'important with regard to marriage.' However it is equally essential and valid for the (understanding) of man in general: for the fundamental problem of understanding him and for the self-understanding of his being in the world."

—Christopher West, Theology of the Body

We, as Christ followers, must recapture this Biblical thinking of the spiritual and physical together in whom we are created and recreated to be, in Christ! "Created in His image," "male and female He created them," "the two shall become one flesh," and "The Word became flesh" are all central to God's design and His Gospel message that we must share in how we live and relate in honoring our spirit and body, along with His message that "marriage should be honored by all" (Hebrews 13:4). Only as we bring all of His Truth together in word and deeds can we reach a world enslaved to the enemy's lies to destroy all of God's design and order and Christ's restoration and redemption of all Creation.

CHAPTER 30

SERPENTS & DOVES...
TAKING HIS MESSAGE
TO THE WORLD

"Behold, I send you forth as sheep in the midst of wolves.
Be ye therefore wise as serpents and harmless as doves."

— Matthew 10:16

In our fast food, internet-driven world, discipline and patience are almost afterthoughts. We "train" our new church converts in a four- to eight-week class, call it discipleship, and send them out to show others how much God loves them, how much we love them, and to win their souls for Christ! On the other hand, Jesus, knowing His time for ministry was short, was not willing to send out His disciples until they were ready. He spent two of the three years of His public ministry training His disciples. He then gave them the encouragement and warning found in Matthew 10:16 (KJ21), "Behold, I send you out as sheep in the midst of wolves. Therefore be wise as serpents and harmless as doves."

How are we doing when it comes to sending out wise and shrewd messengers and disciples?

There are many issues we as a country, and even through our churches, have exported around the globe with horrific consequences. The culture, through our education and government, has co-opted the Gospel message, couching it in familiar terms but exporting death and destruction. Abortion couched in human rights language; contraception in terms of health, well-being, and sexual rights; and pornography labeled as free speech. The Church has done little to counter the messages and in some cases has helped spread the demoralizing and devastating outcomes.

Much of what has been shared from western progressivism has elevated unhealthy relationships and sexual immorality disguising them as education and legislation. Not content to let others decide for themselves, we have forced other cultures and countries to comply through financial incentives or held them hostage with financial restrictions, such as withholding government funding for HIV-AIDS or other program funding if they will not agree to teach and promote condom and contraception-based sex education.

When we comply, by consent or silence, we are allowing the enemy to attack the very foundations of God's creation and order.

I'm focusing on this area because this is the core issue and the greatest ammunition the enemy has in destroying the foundations that God laid down at creation. In His design, male and female were created for marriage in a lifetime monogamous covenant commitment and sex is reserved for this union only. When porn is disguised as "education" and deceitfully marketed as "safe," it goes directly against all that is God and His Truth and Love.

As stated earlier, porn/porneia is the greatest destroyer of love and relationship and the power of the Gospel lived out through His families and Church is the only thing that will overcome it.

If we are going to re-establish the foundations of God's Word in marriage, family, and His Church then we must expose and stand firm against this evil. We must be as wise as serpents and as gentle as doves.

Exporting Porn & "Churchianity"

In 1991 I was asked to join a few other folks to meet with Pastor Shu of the underground church in China. After four hours of listening to him, we each had the opportunity to ask one question. Needless to say, he'd heard them all.

As last to ask, I pulled the reporter's trick and combined two questions into one, "How can we help and what can we learn from you?"

Pastor Shu had spent no more than one minute on the other questions and did the same with my first, "We don't need you to teach us how to do church. We need money and Bibles." He then talked for nearly 30 minutes answering the second question.

He said, "The American Church needs to learn humility. You look at the buildings and numbers, your missionary outreach, and count those as success and think The Lord is blessing you. Well, He has, but God is taking His hands off the American Church." You could hear a pin drop.

He continued to explain, "For the first 20 or so years (mid-60s to mid-80s) when our young men wanted to enter into the ministry/pastorate, we would send them to your Bible colleges and seminaries, to your Christian families and churches. Over time almost every one of them returned full of pornography and materialism. Their marriages and families would fall apart. The more western culture we got, including 'church,' the more we were losing our young men, marriages, and families! How could they do ministry and how could our churches survive in this way?"

Continuing, he said, "Now, when our young men seek out the ministry, we tell them they have to gather the four Gospels (may take several months or years) and memorize all of them before even being considered. When we began to do this, Christ's Church in China began to thrive. Now you see why we need Bibles and money and why The American Church needs humility."

A few years later Ami and I began a young couples' class that grew to over 100 in the first six months. It was through this class and the Sexual Risk Avoidance program that I mentioned in the Introduction that The Lord began to develop the message now known as Love & Lordship. It was continuing to become clear that The Lord had us on this path to help build Godly hearts, homes, and His Church and Kingdom.

The enemy uses porneia to destroy lives, relationships, and communities through divorce and broken families. This hinders our ability to serve the Church, and ultimately cripples its ministry. Most of it is exported from a pornified culture rooted in Churchianity!

How can our churches survive if we continue to placate the culture? What was and is being exported is what is prevalent in our churches today.

"It would seem that Our Lord finds our desires not too strong, but too weak. We are half-hearted creatures, fooling about with drink and sex and ambition when infinite joy is offered us, like an ignorant child who wants to go on making mud pies in a slum because he cannot imagine what is meant by the offer of a holiday at the sea. We are far too easily pleased."

— C.S. Lewis, *The Weight of Glory*

Current Outcomes/Potential Struggles – Present & Eternal

It is obvious there are several issues we need to address to stand against what the world and enemy of our souls is pandering. We need to boldly, yet graciously, step up and proclaim God's Truth. As Abraham Kuyper stated, "There is not a square inch in the whole domain of our human existence over which Christ, who is Sovereign over all, does not cry, 'Mine!'"

Why have we, as Christ's Church, timidly allowed the world to dictate when and where His Truth can be spoken and applied? It is the only thing that will set people free, but we claim graciousness in withholding His Word in politics, schools, media and more while Satan continues to enslave.

Paul said: "For God has not given us a spirit of timidity, but of power and love and discipline." (1 Timothy 1:7 NASB) Here are some outcomes that give evidence to our fear and timidity.

- Emotionally-driven salvation
- Very lacking in obedience-based discipleship
- Spiritually immature, fleshly driven service
- Focus on people above God
- Churches and Christians that look and act like the culture

All of these have been addressed throughout this book as a response to Jesus' own prophecy of Judgment Day in Matthew 7:21-23: "Not everyone who says to Me, 'Lord, Lord,' will enter the kingdom of heaven, but he who does the will of My Father who is in heaven will enter. Many will say to Me on that day, 'Lord, Lord, did we not prophesy in Your name, and in Your name cast out demons, and in Your name perform many miracles?' And then I will declare to them, 'I never knew you; DEPART FROM ME, YOU WHO PRACTICE LAWLESSNESS.'"

The only thing we have any control over in this prophecy is whether we are contributing to the "many" whom Jesus refers to or working to diminish the "many" that don't really know Him!

> *"When the foundations are destroyed,*
> *what can the righteous do?"*
>
> — Psalm 11:3

In answering the Psalmist's question, our focus will be on the issue of porneia or sexual immorality although there are many problems facing our churches today. This permeates our culture and directly attacks the foundations for marriage, family and loving relationships. We will take a 30,000-foot view of the current state of marriage, family and the church. We will see how the lies and deception permeate our systems, destroying God's design for gender, relationships, sexuality, marriage and family and cripple His Church.

We will look at the predominant responses of today's churches. Finally I will present an obedience-based discipleship approach that begins in the home and migrates into the Church to stand against these schemes and attacks from Satan.

CHAPTER 31

WHO'S DISCIPLING OUR YOUTH?

Whoever trains our children will have their hearts and minds. Remember, we are commanded to be diligent in training up our children in what we provide for them and what we protect them from. –Deuteronomy 6:4-9; Proverbs 22:6; Ephesians 6:4

Here's a visual of the current paradigm as peddled by Planned Parenthood, Sexuality Information and Education Council of the United States (SIECUS) and Advocates for Youth (AFY). They set themselves up with compassionate and expert sounding names to draw people into their lies and deceptions while preaching and teaching their brand of relationships and sexuality apart from God's Word. Their message is rooted in "free sex" and promoted and encouraged through condom promotion, porn disguised as "sex education," and abortion, with devastation and death left in the wake.

FRUIT OF THE CURRENT PARADIGM–
CONFORMED TO THE WORLD–REAPING WHAT WE'VE SOWN
Romans 12:2: Galatians 6:7-8

Fruits

Divorce   Fatherless Homes

Teen/Unwed Pregnancies

Depression

Suicidal Tendencies

Abortion

Addiction

Cohabitation

Promiscuity STDs

Pornography

Roots/Foundation

Planned Parenthood/SIECUS/AFY–Condom Promotion,
Free Sex Education 70%+ Of Today's Youth

In the image above, the blackened leaves and fruit coming from the roots and teachings represent promiscuity, porn, depression, cohabitation, abortion, STDs, teen/unwed pregnancies, divorce, broken homes and much more, all a direct attack on God's foundation and order.

We learned earlier that in Proverbs 22:6 the Hebrew word for "train up" means to "bend or shape" and it applies to whoever is doing the "discipling or teaching." Those who are sowing the "seeds of destruction" here in The U.S. are "discipling" with this message internationally through USAIDS dollars and their condom-promotion, free sex agenda. BEWARE!

Again, I ask the question, "Who's discipling our youth?" Let's BE STRONG in standing in God's Truth and sharing His Word to remind others that God alone can take what's wrong and make it right. (Joel 2:25)

> *"Do I believe that God can deal with my 'yesterday,' and make it as though It had never been? I either do not believe he can, or I do not want Him to. Forgiveness, which is so easy for us to accept, cost God the agony of Calvary. When Jesus Christ says, 'Sin no more,' He conveys the power that enables a man not to sin any more, and that power comes by right of what He did on the Cross."*

— Oswald Chambers, *Still Higher for His Highest*

Current Church Paradigm:
Conformed to the World/Reaping What Is Sown

Romans 12:2 states that we are not to conform to the world and Galatians 6:7-8 remind us that the outcome of doing so is that we will reap what we sow.

The following graphic is what the efforts and fruit look like as the modern church has implemented its strategies and programs.

"Make a tree good and its fruit will be good, or make a tree bad and its fruit will be bad, for a tree is recognized by its fruit." — Matthew 12:33

FRUIT OF THE CURRENT PARADIGM –
CONFORMED TO THE WORLD-REAPING WHAT WE'VE SOWN
Romans 12:2; Galatians 6:7-8

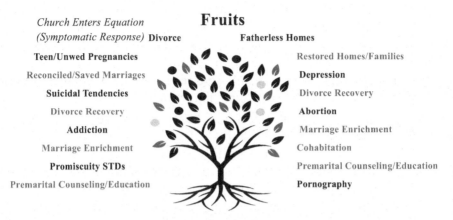

Fruits

Church Enters Equation
(Symptomatic Response) Divorce   Fatherless Homes

Church Enters Equation	Fruits
Teen/Unwed Pregnancies	Restored Homes/Families
Reconciled/Saved Marriages	Depression
Suicidal Tendencies	Divorce Recovery
Divorce Recovery	Abortion
Addiction	Marriage Enrichment
Marriage Enrichment	Cohabitation
Promiscuity STDs	Premarital Counseling/Education
Premarital Counseling/Education	Pornography

Roots/Foundation
Planned Parenthood/SIECUS/AFY – Condom Promotion,
Free Sex Education 70%+ Of Today's Youth

Churches enter with a symptomatic response of some great programs—marriage prep, enrichment, mentoring, reconciliation, divorce recovery, possibly Sexual Risk Avoidance—that teach and encourage abstinence and building healthy relationships. This results in some saved marriages and restored families, but far too many are still exposed to the filth and immorality of the "free sex" programs and reap the consequences.

How often have our classes, programs and ministries, even with the greatest intentions, fallen flat because we have either ignored His priorities and order or we have been blinded to them and based our success on numbers? When they fail we have to come up with a new class, ministry, or program to keep the excitement rather than encourage, test, and hold accountable those relationships built on His Truths.

The fruit in this current paradigm remains overwhelmingly bad because the seeds sown are bad; therefore, Scripturally, we must reap destruction as we pluck a few out of it.

The bad seeds are sown several hours weekly or even daily in schools and exponentially multiplied as they direct youth and children to their internet presence. Contrast that with combating the message with church programs that may add up to a few hours annually in youth group or a sermon or two.

I believe that these are done with great hearts and intent, but the real question is, "Are they working?" We may "rescue" a few from the dangers and consequences of immoral relationships and sexuality, but the enemy's message continues to reach thousands more through the schools, internet, and media. Unless we change the paradigm to obedience-based discipleship in loving relationships we will continue to win a few hearts and lose many, many more.

Yes, it requires diligence, but it will be worth it as we see marriages, homes, and families that are the building blocks of His Bride and Family, the Church. Then because of the life- infusing examples of marriages and loving, Godly relationships, the world will clamor for this kind of love! There are good examples and some wonderful relationships out there, but the reality is that in our churches and certainly in the larger culture there is a glaring absence.

I don't think it's because we don't care. I think it's because, in our desire to see people saved, we've "redesigned" His order to draw people in to hear the Gospel message. However, the enemy has taken full advantage of our heartfelt but misplaced priorities when it comes to expecting obedience, building loving relationships, and making disciples. (John 14:15, 21; 1 Peter 1:22; 1 John 2:5; 5:2)

"Does the Lord delight in burnt offerings and sacrifices as much as in obeying the Lord? To obey is better than sacrifice, and to heed is better than the fat of rams. For rebellion is like the sin of divination, and arrogance like the evil of idolatry. Because you have rejected the word of the Lord, He has rejected you as king." (1 Samuel 15:22–23)

There's a better way and it is found in God's Word and is the very essence of this book. Obedience-based discipleship under Christ's teaching in our families with churches stepping up to reinforce the messages and help encourage obedience and accountability with grace and Truth! Strengthen the family and we all win!

The "New" Old Paradigm:
His Loving Discipleship in Relationships

Check out this visual of what this "new" paradigm may look like in line with obedience-based discipleship in our homes and churches...

"CUNNING AS SERPENTS, GENTLE AS DOVES"
Matthew 10:16

Healthy Marriages   **Fruits**   **Healthy Families**

Divorce   Fatherless Homes

Teen/Unwed Pregnancies   Vibrant Churches

Reconciled/Saved Marriages   Depression

Suicidal Tendencies   Divorce Recovery

Divorce Recovery   Abortion

Addiction   Restored Homes/Families

Marriage Enrichment   Cohabitation

Promiscuity STDs   Addiction Recovery

Premarital Counseling/Education   Pornography

Marriage Mentoring

Roots/Foundation
Marriage and Family/Discipleship
Truth Foundation in Homes

The Church in partnership with marriages/families to work at the root cause and lay a firm foundation for future success.

Now we begin to see the healthy fruit of loving relationships built on His Love and Lordship and our obedient discipleship. Remember in the current paradigm more than 70% are receiving an immoral and rotten seed. What kind of impact would obedience-based discipleship have on your church? What impact would your church have in your community?

CHAPTER 32

CHANGING THE PARADIGM: TRANSFORMED BY RENEWING OUR MINDS

Reaching a lost world begins with our own changed lives by the grace and salvation of Christ.

He calls us to a new life with changed hearts and minds that no longer live for the selfish flesh and desires but for His Kingdom and glory.

This is done through real discipleship under His Lordship where He takes priority over every aspect of our lives. In order to gain our lives we must lose them to Him (Luke 9:24). We also must understand that we are called to obedience as His disciples and as we mature in His Word and Spirit we take His message of new life to a lost and dying world. That's why Jesus came.

Why Love & Lordship Authority (The Author's Design)

Lordship (Authority)

Discipleship

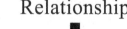

Relationship

⬇

Sin/Issues/Problems

In order to truly change and deal with the sin in our personal and relational lives and help those who are lost, we must make Him Lord and walk as His disciples!

This ultimately means that we cannot assume that those in the world around us, or even those who sit in our churches, understand His Love and Lordship (Authority). It is imperative that we understand His Word, that he reigns in our lives, and our desire is that we share it with others by word and deed.

Look around, folks. We're not getting the message of his Love and Lordship or passing it on as disciples making disciples.

This must change! Christ's prophetic warning in Matthew 7:21–23 has everything to do with a right relationship with Him that is then lived out and observed by the world in our relationships, first in our families and then in His Church. We must truly receive by His grace through faith (Ephesians 2:8-9), and then strive to live out this priority relationship with Him (Philippians 2:12-13). This is what gives us His Authority in the lives of others as they will see it and invite us to have influence in their lives—True Authority lived out in Love!

We will not crumble because bogus and pseudo rights are not being protected, rather we will crumble with the lawless, immoral and unethical continuation of so-called "rights." Every global power that has existed and subsequently collapsed did so from the moral collapse within – and every bit of it was posited as something good, right or moral – actually to mask the indulgent, selfish and pleasurable! How stubborn or downright blind do we need to be to see that the exact same immoralities posed as moral, right and good are deteriorating our culture and society today? It is evident in every part of our culture – government, media, education, religion (church) and home/family! Who will stand for the Truth about right, good and morality? That is who will either make a difference or be persecuted for trying and in the end will be proven right!

God's Covenant Design

Why is this important? We must remember that God's design from the beginning moves from the individual to the relational (marriage and family) into the community (Church) and finally into systems (governments and nations).

When we fail to build up strong disciples and loving relationships in our homes, the best we can do, even with the greatest of intentions, is create a façade of systems that will ultimately enslave. Even our churches then become primarily a system of programs and governance rather than a loving and united fellowship and family of believers. That's why God began with a marriage and a family!

This Truth of His Love and Lordship has never changed.

174

STUDY GUIDE
WISE AS SERPENTS,
GENTLE AS DOVES

Key Concepts

1) We must be prepared as Christ's disciples to take His message to the world.

2) Preparation calls for us to be studied, obedient, wise and gracious.

3) Modern day outcomes include emotionally based "salvation," a lack of obedience-based discipleship, spiritual immaturity and fleshly driven service.

4) Cultural Christianity places emphasis on people above God.

5) Restoring the foundations of Lordship, discipleship, Godly marriage, families, and relationships is essential to reviving The Church.

6) The greatest destroyer of loving relationships is sexual immorality or porneia.

7) The culture spreads the "safe sex" message of porneia as perfectly fine, disguised as "education."

8) The fruit of the sexual revolution in our families, churches and culture is immorality and destruction as we are reaping what we have sown.

9) The churches' response is predominantly symptomatic.

10) The Church needs to respond with the foundational principles of relational integrity and sexual purity within marriages and families, with churches and families then supporting each other in obedience-based discipleship and accountability.

11) God's order is to move from the individual to relationships to community to corporate or systemic. If we do not heed His Word with individuals and in relationships, we will not be able to spread it in our communities or systems.

12) The Scriptural paradigm of the Love and Lordship message Lordship⇨Discipleship⇨Relationships⇨Sin/Issues Problems.

Key Questions

1) What has been your experience in learning about relationships and sexuality?

2) What have you learned about how you can make a difference in building loving relationships?

3) What will you do differently as a spouse or parent with regard to discipleship and relationships?

4) What have you learned that you can apply to your church family?

5) What insights have you gained regarding God's Covenant Order?

6) How might this change your life, family, church life, and outreach to others?

Discussion

1) What does it mean for Christ to be Lord of your life? Your marriage? Your family?

2) How about Lord of your Church?

3) Discuss the concept of God's working from the individual through relationships and community to impact our culture and systems.

4) What do you need to do to show His Love and Lordship in every part of your life?

MARRIAGE/FAMILY
MINISTRIES & RESOURCES

WEBSITES

Grace Marriage: www.gracemarriage.com
Marriage Savers: www.marriagesavers.org
FamilyLife: www.familylife.com
All Pro Dad: www.allprodad.com
American Family Association: afa.net
Focus on the Family: www.focusonthefamily.com
Homeword: www.homeword.com
Pure Life Ministries: www.purelifeministries.org
Faithful and True: www.faithfulandtrue.com
L.I.F.E. Ministries International: www.freedomeveryday.org
Marriage Today: www.marriagetoday.com
MERCY: www.mercyky.org

MOVIES

Fireproof: www.kendrickbrotherscatalogue.com/fireproof
Courageous: www.kendrickbrotherscatalogue.com/courageous
War Room: www.kendrickbrotherscatalogue.com/warroom/home
Overcomer: www.kendrickbrotherscatalogue.com/overcomer
Like Arrows: www.familylife.com/likearrows

BOOKS

Love and Respect by Emerson Eggerichs
Uncompromised Faith by S. Michael Craven
Kingdom Man and Kingdom Marriage by Dr. Tony Evans
His Needs, Her Needs by Willard Harley
His Needs, Her Needs for Parents by Willard Harley
Sacred Marriage by Gary Thomas
Sacred Parenting by Gary Thomas
Cherish by Gary Thomas
The Five Love Languages by Gary Chapman
Parenting by the Book by John Rosemond
What He Must Be...if he wants to marry my daughter by Dr. Voddie Baucham
A Chicken's Guide to Talking Turkey with Your Kids About Sex by Dr. Kevin Leman
Questions Kids Ask About Sex edited by Melissa Cox

Ami & Greg Williams

Greg Williams is the Director of Love & Lordship and former President/CEO of Heritage of KY. Married to Ami Haid Williams. They have three children, Lansing, Harrison and Haidyn.

Greg earned his BA in Accounting from Transylvania University, Lexington, KY; his BA, Business Education from the University of Kentucky, Lexington; and his MA in Secondary Education from Georgetown College, Georgetown, KY.

He is/has been on the Board of Directors of Soteria Network, Initiatives, Inc.; Women for Life (Assurance); FamilyNet and Building Healthy Marriages Partnership; Commonwealth Marriage

Initiative Task Force; Healthy Relationship Skills Ministry Team for the Association for Marriage and Family Ministries.

Greg hosted Character Matters, a Cable TV show for Fayette County Public Schools; Character Minute radio spots to encourage character understanding/development; and co-hosted with Ami Marriage Unleashed, a guest talk show focused on healthy marriage on WTVQ Channel 36 (Lexington, KY, ABC affiliate).

Love & Lordship is a result of churches, couples and individuals seeking a deeper relationship with Christ and a desire to see the effects of this priority relationship on every part of their personal lives, relationships, marriage and family, as well as the Church and culture. Love & Lordship events present a solid Biblical approach to relationships, sexuality, marriage and family and the impact we are called to have in and through Christ's Church. Greg has spoken to tens of thousands at numerous men's, women's, and marriage events across the U.S., and as the keynote presenter at the International Marriage and Family Conference in Cameroon, West Africa.

Ami Williams is a transplant to Lexington, having been born in Michigan and raised in northern Ohio. Ami moved to Lexington during middle school, graduated from Lafayette High School, and then received a BA in Journalism from the University of Kentucky. She worked in television news as a reporter and producer at LEX18 after graduation.

After taking a career break to have her three children, Ami returned to journalistic pursuits as a copyright specialist and editor at Southland Christian Church. During this time she also served as managing editor for a local magazine, Lexington Woman, and worked for Lexington Family Magazine as a writer and proofreader.

For the last several years Ami has worked in communications for private schools in Lexington that their children attended.

"

Greg is a passionate voice for Christian marriages. As the family goes, so goes the church. I never enjoyed weddings but I loved to see Christian marriages because they are the building blocks of society. Greg can encourage your church and couples and help bear the load if you let him use what he has learned.

— Wayne B. Smith (1929-2016), Founder/Senior Minister, Southland Christian Church, Lexington, KY

The Authority of Love and the foundation of God's Truth that it stands on are desperately needed, as we see people being devoured by today's culture. Under Greg Williams' leadership and gifted speaking ability, we have been challenged and reminded to live our lives in a way that glorifies God each time we have hosted Love & Lordship event. The passion that Greg and the ministry have to make a difference in the lives of all Christ followers is something we all should strive for.

— Greg Horn, HOPE is Here Host, Lexington, KY

My wife and I had the privilege of attending Greg's 7-session Love and Lordship event held at our church. Those sessions were extremely well done and everyone from our church loved them. I've since used some of his materials in my pre-marriage counseling sessions. Greg's passion for marriage and the family lights up the stage. We were so impressed with that first event that we had Greg come back and lead one of our church-wide group sessions as well. This book will be a great tool for those looking to fulfill God's covenant design for marriage and family.

— Terry Cooper, Senior Minister, Ninevah Christian Church, Lawrenceburg, KY

"

I want to recommend to you 'The Authority of Love' by Greg Williams. Greg came and shared these Biblical principles at our church several years ago. I know that you will be challenged and encouraged by Greg's approach to having a Bible-based marriage. The root of our problem is often a result of our not being intimate with Jesus or not hearing Him in a specific area of our life. Greg will spur you on to get you into His Word and apply it to that aspect of your marriage.

I believe that if you will apply the truths that Greg will share with you in this book, not only will your marriage be stronger but so will your personal walk with Christ.

— Herb Williams, Lead Pastor, New Hope Community Church, Elizabethtown, KY

It is clear that the Lord's strong hand is upon Greg Williams, to teach Love & Lordship. His presentation is biblically sound and he speaks the truth in love! His passion for this God-given assignment shines through and it makes the teaching even more compelling! We are being educated on a deeper level, about Love, Lordship and marriage. Every one of our lives has truly been transformed as a result!!!

Sisters For Life has received one testimony after another about how the Love & Lordship teaching has changed the way they see marriage and parenting. One lady, who was contemplating divorce, is rethinking her decision. Another couple was having trouble in their marriage, as a result of Greg's teaching, the love they have for the Lord has grown stronger and the love for each other has been rekindled.

I must add that one of the many things I found most impressive about Greg is his ability to relate to everyone in the room!!!

— Angela Minter, Sisters for Life, Louisville, KY

"

Love & Lordship has taught me the importance of living my marriage centered in Christ. I've learned that being the spiritual leader of my family while serving my wife is pleasing to God and honors Him. Love & Lordship has been a significant part of me enjoying and growing my marriage to honor God.

— Jeff Hancock, Lexington, KY

Greg Williams led my wife and I through the Love & Lordship message when our lives were spiraling out of control. His wisdom and guidance led by The Holy Spirit helped save our marriage. We acknowledge the Biblical truth that Greg spoke into our marriage helped us to overcome our unfaithfulness to each other and to God. When the world told us to divorce, Greg told us to repent and save our commitment that we made to each other many years ago. Since then, we have been blessed with 10 years of a renewed life, a redeemed marriage and two beautiful kids. Greg helped us turn our mess into our message. As we reflect, we are eternally thankful that God led us to Greg during our adversity.

— Clif and Stacey Marshall, Bloomington, IN

The Lord is using Greg and the Love & Lordship Ministry in tremendous ways! My wife and I first met Greg at the Love & Lordship conference that was hosted by our church. The two-day seminar was powerful! Never have I met someone with such passion and enthusiasm for healthy marriages and families. He's a hard-hitter, sometimes the content is tough, challenging and convicting but I can truthfully say that Greg used the Word of God to breathe new life into my marriage.

Our church body was so blessed by the Love & Lordship conference that we didn't think twice about bringing Greg back as the keynote speaker for our Men's Retreat.

— Chris and Amanda Tucker, Winchester, KY

"

The traditional American family is under assault and getting weaker by the day. Restoring it to its original purpose and function will only happen by highly intentional effort. Greg Williams provides key instruction and motivation for men to become diligent disciples, humble husbands and faithful fathers. A relevant and powerful message presented in a clear and effective way.

Expect to be radically changed from the inside out!

— Kent Laufenburger, Lexington, KY

This was the best material I have heard and I have a masters of divinity in pastoral counseling from Southern Baptist Seminary. Right on the money. Convicting and liberating. I've been telling everyone about the teaching. I wish I had been trained to teach and live this as I attended seminary...would have saved a lot of heartache, mine and others.

— James Driver, Frankfort, KY

For countless generations the family has been under attack but maybe not as complete as what our society faces today. The enemy wishes to steal, kill and destroy and time is short. I am thankful for Greg and his ministry, which is devoted to the health of marriages and families. Inside you will not only find timeless principles of truth but solid counsel to help make your family not only withstand, but excel during these troublesome times.

— Jeff Rogers, Director of Wellspring Prayer Center

For more information and to
have Greg Williams speak at your
church or organization, contact
Love & Lordship at
loveandlordship@gmail.com.

www.loveandlordship.com
On Facebook and Twitter
@LoveandLordship
Also on Apple Podcast, Google Play, YouTube and Vimeo